270 | 280 | 290 | 300 | 310 | 320 | 330 | 340 | 350

60

BAFFINS BAY

ARCTICK LAND

DAVIS STRAITS

NEW NORTH WALES

50

HUDSONS BAY

NEW SOUTH WALES

NEW BRITAIN

NEW FOUND LAND

The Main Bank

James Bay

L. Piscoutagami

NEW FRANCE

LAKE SUPERIOR

Falls Bank

of Land
Wild Bulls

40

LAKE HURONS

LAKE ERIE

PENN

MAR
IRGI
NIA

CAPE COD

SEA OF THE ENGLISH EMPIRE

30

Bermudez als Summer Iland

THE GOLF OR
BAY OF
MEXICO

BAHAMA ISLANDS

ANTILLES Iˢ **WEST INDIAN**

20

SEA
CARIBY
ISLANDS

YUCATAN

HONDURAS

10

· VOICES ·
from
COLONIAL AMERICA

NEW HAMPSHIRE

1603 — 1776

SCOTT AUDEN

WITH

ALAN TAYLOR, PH.D., CONSULTANT

NATIONAL GEOGRAPHIC

WASHINGTON, D.C.

Text copyright © 2007 National Geographic Society
Published by the National Geographic Society.
All rights reserved. Reproduction of the whole or any part of the contents without written permission from the National Geographic Society is strictly prohibited. For information about special discounts for bulk purchases, please contact National Geographic Books Special Sales: ngspecsales@ngs.org

John M. Fahey, Jr., *President and Chief Executive Officer*
Gilbert M. Grosvenor, *Chairman of the Board*
Nina D. Hoffman, *Executive Vice President, President Book Publishing Group*

STAFF FOR THIS BOOK

Nancy Laties Feresten, *Vice President, Editor-in-Chief of Children's Books*
Amy Shields, *Executive Editor, Children's Books*
Suzanne Patrick Fonda, *Project Editor*
Robert D. Johnston, Ph.D., *Associate Professor and Director, Teaching of History Program University of Illinois at Chicago, Series Editor*
Bea Jackson, *Director of Design and Illustration, Children's Books*
Jean Cantu, *Illustrations Specialist*
Carl Mehler, *Director of Maps*
Justin Morrill, *The M Factory, Inc., Map Research, Design, and Production*
Rebecca Baines, *Editorial Assistant*
Jennifer Thornton, *Managing Editor*
Connie D. Binder, *Indexer*
R. Gary Colbert, *Director, Production and Managing Editorial*
Lewis R. Bassford, *Production Manager*
Nicole Elliott and Maryclare Tracy, *Manufacturing Managers*

Voices from Colonial New Hampshire was prepared by CREATIVE MEDIA APPLICATIONS, INC.

Scott Auden, *Writer*
Fabia Wargin Design, Inc., *Design and Production*
Susan Madoff, *Editor*
Laurie Lieb, *Copyeditor*
Cindy Joyce, *Image Researcher*

Body text is set in Deepdene, sidebars are Caslon 337 Oldstyle, and display text is Cochin Archaic Bold.

LIBRARY OF CONGRESS CATALOGING-IN-PUBLICATION DATA
Auden, Scott.
    New Hampshire, 1603-1776 / by Scott Auden.
        p. cm. — (Voices from colonial America)
    Includes bibliographical references and index.
    ISBN 978-1-4263-0034-9 (trade : alk. paper)
    ISBN 978-1-4263-0035-6 (library : alk. paper)
    1. New Hampshire—History—Colonial period, ca. 1600-1775—Juvenile literature.   I. Title.
    F37.A93 2007
    974.2'02—dc22

                                        2006036055

Printed in Belgium

CONTENTS

INTRODUCTION 9

CHAPTER ONE:
The Stage Is Set 13

CHAPTER TWO:
Planting of the Piscataqua 25

CHAPTER THREE:
Massachusetts Gains Control 37

CHAPTER FOUR:
Royal New Hampshire 49

CHAPTER FIVE:
Life in New Hampshire 57

CHAPTER SIX:
Life Under the Lords of Trade 69

CHAPTER SEVEN:
A Time of Growth 81

CHAPTER EIGHT:
Revolutionary New Hampshire....................91

TIME LINE 104

RESOURCES 105

QUOTE SOURCES 106

INDEX 107

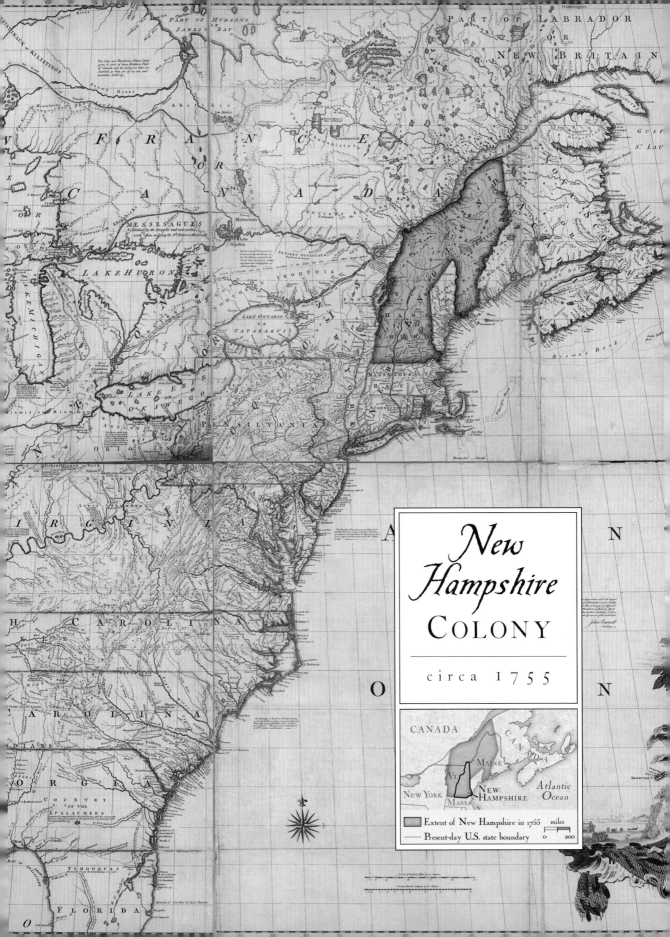

INTRODUCTION

by

Alan Taylor, Ph.D.

The *Ranger*, commissioned by the Continental Navy for the
Revolutionary War, was built in Portsmouth, New Hampshire in 1777.
The ship was captured by the British in 1780 and renamed H.M.S. *Halifax*.

New Hampshire seems so pleasant and peaceful: a beautiful
place to live and to visit. The craggy White Mountains,
rolling hills, and pounding ocean all suggest a timeless
beauty. The graceful buildings that survive from the colonial
past also evoke comfort and dignity. Visit Strawbery Banke
in Portsmouth or the nearby Wentworth mansion, and it is
easy to think of the colonial past as quaint and gracious:

OPPOSITE: This historical map, created by John Mitchell in 1755, has been
colorized for this book to emphasize the boundaries of the New Hampshire
colony. The inset map shows the state's present-day boundaries for comparison.

a time of ladies in gowns and gentlemen in wigs. But present looks can deceive about the past.

In fact, as Scott Auden's book reveals, the people of colonial New Hampshire had to overcome great hardships and dangers, some of them self-inflicted. Indeed, they waged three great struggles against long odds. First, they had to support themselves while figuring out how to live in a demanding environment. Second, they fought to conquer that land from native peoples defending their own way of life. And third, the newcomers had to fend off a powerful neighbor: the larger and aggressive colony of Massachusetts. All three struggles were related.

Compared to most of the other colonies, New Hampshire was a cold, northern land with a dense forest and a stony soil. The newcomers labored long, hard days to cut the trees, chop firewood, erect fences, build barns and houses, and to plow and plant fields between the stumps. They had to do all this from scratch with hand tools and some oxen. Between the last frost of spring and the first of late summer, the climate offered a dangerously short growing season for grains. And the colonists had to harvest enough hay to feed their animals—cattle, sheep, and horses— through the long, dark, and cold winter.

They called this demanding land a "wilderness," but it had belonged for centuries to Indians who lived by a combination of farming, fishing, hunting, and gathering. At first, the natives welcomed the newcomers as a few traders, but the Indians soon resented losing more land as many more colonists came to make farms. Driven away from the coast, most of the Indians sought refuge in the mountains, or farther north, in Canada. There they made allies with the French, who helped them attack the settlements of New Hampshire, burning dozens of homes, killing many colonists, and taking many more prisoner.

Limited in number, the New Hampshire colonists needed military help from Massachusetts. But that help came with strings attached. During the 1650s, Massachusetts took control of Maine, the colony east of New Hampshire with a similar frontier problem. That takeover made the leaders of Massachusetts more eager to grab New Hampshire, too—as the price for providing troops to defend the frontier and to attack Indian villages.

How did the people of New Hampshire preserve their colony? This is the question that author Scott Auden answers in this book. Although specific to New Hampshire, his answers help us to understand how the colonial experience shaped the new nation created by the American Revolution.

The first state seal of New Hampshire, designed in 1776, features a fish, a bundle of five arrows, and a pine tree. The fish and pine tree represent the state's most important resources, and the arrows symbolize unity among the five counties settled at the time of statehood.

CHAPTER ONE

The Stage Is Set

In 1603, Englishman Martin Pring reaches the Piscataqua River and spends time exploring the region.

Europeans living in the 16th century were in awe of the Spanish Empire in Central and South America with its Aztec and Inca gold. The Spaniards had found great success by conquering and making slaves of the native populations in order to exploit the regions' natural resources. Other European empires were interested in matching Spain's success and looked to explore areas where the Spanish had not yet ventured. Vikings from Scandinavia had journeyed as far as Newfoundland, but the parts of North America that are now the United States and

OPPOSITE: A Native American builds a birch-bark canoe along a waterway in New Hampshire. The Indian uses roots to attach bark stripped from nearby birch trees to the frame of the canoe.

Canada remained mostly unknown to Europe. Of course, for many thousands of native men, women, and children, New Hampshire was home. In the race to claim land for empire, Europeans set out for this New World and were introduced to the people living there.

NEW HAMPSHIRE NATIVES

The native people who lived throughout New England and eastern Canada belonged to a group called the Algonquian. Many Algonquian tribes spoke similar languages. Within Algonquian culture, the

New England—name for the region east of New Netherland (New York) that was colonized by England

largest unit of organization was the tribe. A tribe might have as many as 2,000 members. The tribe was led by a sachem and within a tribe were bands. A band was an extended family or group of families, often identified by an animal symbol such as a bear or a wolf. This band lived, hunted, and farmed together. The Algonquian peoples moved from place to place depending on the season and whether they found good hunting or fishing. In addition to the scattered campsites of the different bands, a tribe often had a central village, sometimes with a palisade to protect the members from their enemies. The Indians grew crops at the village and would gather there for planting and harvesting.

palisade—a fence made of sharp sticks, used for defense

The Algonquian peoples lived in round, dome-shaped structures called wigwams. A wigwam's frame was made of saplings and covered with mats made out of bark or woven plant fiber. There was a flap-covered chimney on top and a fire in the center. When it was time to move to a new location, the people left the wigwam frames behind for use on their return.

Although the Algonquians and their ancestors had lived in the New England forests for many centuries, there is some evidence that they were in the midst of a time of change even before the arrival of the Europeans. A few centuries earlier, tribes from the Ohio valley had migrated into Algonquian territory. The Ohio tribes brought with them the secret of working clay to make pottery. Pottery could be used for holding grain, which made food storage much easier than when tribes had been limited to stone vessels. Stone vessels took longer to carve and were heavier and less portable. Carving stone, like hunting, had always been a man's task. When Native American women became experts at making pottery, men of the tribe had more free time. In addition, with more efficient food storage, the men no longer had to hunt as frequently.

anthropologist—
a scientist who studies human beings and their origins, culture, and physical characteristics

According to anthropologists, the Algonquian men, therefore, now had more time to spend as warriors. Conflicts with the Mohawks and the Pequots, two Iroquois tribes, became frequent.

In this illustration, two men observe the activities of a fishing camp in Newfoundland. In the background, men unload the catch from a skiff. Workers on the dock and at tables on the shore filet the fish in preparation for the drying table, which can be seen in the foreground.

THE ARRIVAL OF EUROPEANS

European nations believed that their understanding and control of the seas and distant ports of the New World were vital to trade, and many invested in voyages of discovery.

In 1497, an explorer named John Cabot sailed from Bristol in England to Newfoundland. He may have sailed as far south as New England as well. Newfoundland offered excellent fishing. Fishermen from other nations soon began to visit Newfoundland, camping for weeks on the shore, where they preserved their catch by drying it in the sun before sailing back to Europe with it. Some fishing captains may have sailed south along the coastline, but if any did, no records survive. Ultimately, this temporary European presence in North America was a vital foothold for the later exploration of New England.

Twenty-seven years later, under orders from the King of France, Giovanni da Verrazano landed at what is now North Carolina and then sailed north up the coast. He anchored for two weeks off present-day Newport, Rhode Island. He then continued north past New Hampshire as far as Nova Scotia in what is now eastern Canada, before returning to France. While fishermen continued to visit Newfoundland to fish, and European exploration proceeded far to the south, Europeans neglected the coast in between for the rest of the 16th century.

patent—a grant of land

During the 1560s, under a patent from Queen Elizabeth I of England to develop a colony to be called Virginia, the first English colonists settled briefly at Roanoke in what is now North Carolina. Although the colony failed, the stories that reached England about the attempt fired the imagination.

In 1602, Captain Bartholomew Gosnold sailed his ship, the *Concord*, across the Atlantic to the coast of present-day Maine. He then proceeded south down the coast of New Hampshire. Landing on islands off the coast of Massachusetts, Gosnold and his crew built a small fort, traded with the natives, and collected a valuable cargo of sassafras, a plant the Europeans believed had medicinal value. Upon their return to England, one of the crew members, John Brereton, wrote a book about their journey called *A Brief and True Relation of the Discovery of the North Part of Virginia.*

The Roanoke colony, the popularity of Brereton's *Relation*, and Gosnold's financial success made the exploration of North America very appealing to the English. In 1603, 23-year-old Martin Pring, a sailor from Bristol, led an expedition to North America. His flagship was the 50-ton *Speedwell*, but the expedition also included the 26-ton (24-metric-ton) *Discoverer*. Because it could be rowed and needed much less water beneath its keel, the smaller ship was useful for exploring rivers and coastlines. Some of Pring's crewmen were familiar with the area, having sailed with Gosnold the year before. Reaching present-day

Sassafras

SASSAFRAS IS A TREE NATIVE TO much of North America. It favors sandy soil and grows to be as tall as 150 feet (46 m). It is unusual in that three distinct shapes of leaf grow on the same tree. In the spring, it produces yellow flowers, which develop into egg-shaped fruit sprouting from red-colored cups.

Europeans first learned about sassafras when the Spanish found it growing in Florida. Seventeenth-century Europeans prized the plant, particularly the roots, believing it was a cure for just about any ailment. Even today it has no shortage of uses. Sassafras can be processed into oil for use in perfumes and soaps. It also makes an excellent insect repellent. The roots can be boiled to make tea, and the wood provides a yellow dye. The shoots of the tree provide the flavor in root beer.

Maine, Pring sailed southwest down the coast. After exploring several inlets that *"pierce [jut] not farre [far] into the land,"* he reached the mouth of the Piscataqua River on the coast of New Hampshire.

tidal estuary—a body of water where the outflow of a river meets the ebb and flow of the ocean's tides

The Piscataqua River is a 12-mile-long (19-km) tidal estuary, formed where the Salmon Falls and Cocheco Rivers meet. Captain Pring discovered an excellent harbor where the Piscataqua flows into the sea. Anchored within the harbor, his ships were much safer from the dangers of harsh weather and the rough seas of the Atlantic. In the center of the harbor, he found several islands, the largest called Great Island. About 6 miles (10 km) upriver, just below where the Salmon Falls and Cocheco come together, a broad opening leads to a bay even larger than the harbor he had found. Today it is known as Great Bay.

The Algonquian inhabitants of the area called themselves Abenaki. *Piscataqua* is an Abenaki word that combines the word *peske,* which means "branch," and the word *tegwe,* which describes a river with a strong current. The Abenaki thought of the area as the place where the strong river branches.

Excited to find the wide and inviting harbor, Captain Pring sailed in and anchored the *Speedwell.* Then he went aboard the *Discoverer* to row upriver about 12 miles, exploring the banks and finally turning south and sailing into Great Bay. There his men went ashore to search for sassafras.

FOOLE *and* GALLANT

PRING'S CREW INCLUDED FOOLE and Gallant, two *"great and fearfull Mastives [Mastiffs]."* The Native Americans had no experience with large dogs bred for hunting, and Pring writes that the natives feared the dogs more than 20 of his men. In a practice that would be considered inhumane today, Pring and his men, when they wanted to *"be rid of the Savages company, we would let loose the Mastives, and suddenly with out-cryes they [the natives] would flee away."*

It was June, and the weather was mild. Plants were blooming, and there was wildlife all around them. Pring wrote:

> *we beheld very goodly Groves and Woods replenished with tall O[a]ks, Beeches, Pine-trees, Firre-trees, Hazels, Witch-hazels and Maples. We saw here also sundry sorts of Beasts, [such] as Stags, Deere, Beares, Wolves, Foxes . . . and Dogges with sharpe noses.*

Pring and his men did not find any people. They did discover *"signes of fires where [people] had beene"* and *"certaine Cottages together,"* a reference to Algonquian wig-wams. The explorers came to the conclusion that the dwellings had been *"abandoned by the Savages."* Most of the native people were prob-ably upriver at the waterfalls, where the fishing was good that time of year.

BIRCH-BARK CANOES

ALTHOUGH HE CALLED THEM SAVAGES, MARTIN PRING recognized the Algonquian as master boatbuilders. He was very impressed with their birch-bark canoes and took one back with him to England. He explained:

Their Boats... were seventeen foot long and four foot broad, and made of the Bark of a Birch-tree far exceeding in bigness those of England. It was sowed [sewn] together with strong and tough... twigs, and the seams covered over with Rozen or Turpertine. ...[I]t was also open, ... and sharp at both ends, saving that the beak was a little bending roundly upward. Although it carried nine men standing upright, yet it weighed not at the most above sixty pounds in weight, a thing almost incredible in regard of the largeness and capacity therof. Their Oars were flat at the end... made of Ash or Maple very light and strong, about two yards long, wherewith they row very swiftly.

No boats the Europeans had were so effective on the rivers and lakes of New England.

Near the cottages, the explorers saw crops. Unlike Europeans, Native Americans did not plant different crops in different fields. Instead, various plants were planted together. Beans or other climbing vines might be planted beside corn, for example, where the tall cornstalks served as natural poles for the bean plants to climb. Other plants like squash, would cover the soil and control weeds. Pring wrote,

> We beheld their Gardens . . . one [plant] among the rest [on] an Acre of ground. . . . [I]n the same [acre] was sowne Tobacco, pompions [onions], cowcumbers [cucumbers] and such like; . . . some of the people had Maiz [corn] or Indian Wheate among them. In the fields we found wild Pease, Strawberries very faire and bigge, Gooseberries, Raspices [raspberries] . . . and other wild fruits.

Finding no sassafras, Pring and his crew returned to the *Speedwell* and sailed down the coast. On an island off the coast of Massachusetts, they finally discovered the sassafras they were seeking. Here they decided to stay long enough to gather a cargo of sassafras, replenish their supplies, and plant a test garden to see if European plants were likely to grow in this part of the world. Quickly discovering that the island was inhabited and unsure of the Indians' intentions, they built a small fort to protect themselves from possible attack. Generally, however, they got along well with the island's inhabitants. After several weeks, they filled their ships' holds with the sassafras they collected, fresh supplies and water, furs, and native artifacts, including a birch-bark canoe. Then, on the eighth or ninth of August, they sailed home.

The voyage of the *Speedwell* to the coast of New England in 1603 propelled Pring's career forward. In 1604, shortly after his return to England, he sailed to Guiana on the northern coast of South America. Two years later, he made another voyage to New England, this time exploring the coast of Maine.

Pring took a position with the Dutch East India Company's fleet, the largest trading company at the time. By 1619, he directed the entire English East India fleet. In 1621, he managed a squadron of five ships in the East Indies. At 1,000 tons (907 metric tons), the largest of these ships was more than 20 times the size of the *Speedwell*.

Pring returned to England in 1623, where he died at the age of 46. ✳

CHAPTER TWO

Planting of the Piscataqua

THE COUNCIL OF NEW ENGLAND *is created and distributes patents for land in what is now New Hampshire. Pannaway House, Hilton's Point, and Strawbery Banke become the future colony's first settlements.*

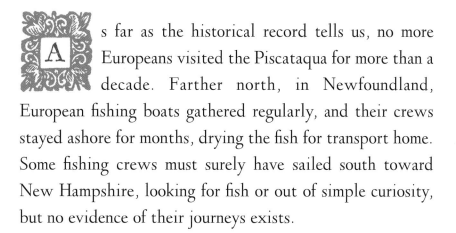

A s far as the historical record tells us, no more Europeans visited the Piscataqua for more than a decade. Farther north, in Newfoundland, European fishing boats gathered regularly, and their crews stayed ashore for months, drying the fish for transport home. Some fishing crews must surely have sailed south toward New Hampshire, looking for fish or out of simple curiosity, but no evidence of their journeys exists.

OPPOSITE: Captain John Smith's map of New England, charting the eastern coastline of North America, is illustrated with the seal of the English Crown and a portrait of the mapmaker. Smith's map was the first to call the region New England.

In 1614, London merchants sent Captain John Smith to the coast of Maine with instructions to catch whales and discover gold mines. Smith traveled southwest down the coast, making a detailed, accurate map. He would write of his trip down the coast: *"Could I have but means to transport a colony, I would rather live here than anywhere."* When he returned to England, he presented his map to Prince Charles.

That map became famous. In the minds of many merchants, the success of the fishing camps in Newfoundland hinted at much greater profit to be made in North America. For one thing, the Native Americans were willing to trade. In return for European blankets, mirrors, iron cookware, and metal tools, the Indians would supply furs, which were valuable back in Europe. Furthermore, the merchants were very interested in the timber that could be cut from the vast, towering forests. But they needed permanent settlements to make it all possible.

EUROPEANS IN THE NEW WORLD

In 1607, the English had established the Jamestown colony in Virginia, and it had managed to grow. In 1620, a group of Puritans established the Plymouth colony near where Martin Pring and his crew had spent the summer 17 years earlier.

Puritan—a Protestant whose faith was based on the Bible rather than the teachings of church leaders.

In the early 1600s, all the English settlements in North America were governed by the Virginia Company. Sir Ferdinando Gorges, the English nobleman who commanded the fort that protected the English seaport of Plymouth, wanted to make a fortune in the New World, but first he had to change the way it was governed. Gorges convinced the king that North America was too vast to be governed by one company. He pushed for the creation of a governing body that would be located in England, but control land and trade in New England. He succeeded, and in 1620, he became president of the newly created Council for New England.

He immediately issued a patent to the settlers of Plymouth for their land. In effect, it gave them permission to keep operating as they had been. Then, for the next two years, he and the other members of the council issued patents to themselves, their friends, and others with enough money or political influence.

One patent went to a 32-year-old Scot named David Thompson, who was a friend of Gorges. He was given 6,000 acres (2,430 ha) of land and a single island of his choice. Early in 1623, Thompson and two friends crossed the Atlantic on the *Jonathan of Plymouth* to settle in Piscataqua in what is now New Hampshire. They arrived in early spring, and during the next three months, a half dozen other men joined their settlement.

From the beginning, the settlement of New Hampshire was a business venture intended to make money. Thompson and the others planned to establish a permanent, year-round presence in the area. They hoped to trade with the Indians, fish, and dry their catch for transport to England. At the end of five years, they would split the profits with their sponsors back in England and keep the land they occupied.

PANNAWAY HOUSE

Thompson's men chose a hill overlooking the rocky shore near the entrance to the harbor, a place the natives called Pannaway, known today as Odiorne's Point. There was a freshwater spring nearby, and the hill offered easy defense and an excellent view of the mouth of the river. They cleared the trees and built a house of pine logs and stone. It was designed like a fort, with mounted guns that could shoot in any direction from within. They also set up wooden racks for drying fish. Well-made and secure, Pannaway House stood for at least 60 years. When it was finished, Thompson sent for his wife and her maid to join him on the plantation.

plantation—a settlement in a new region of colonial America

Because fish, game, timber, and many other natural resources were abundant in North America, Europeans mistakenly believed that it would be easy to live there. Back in England, colonial recruiters encouraged this belief. In 1624, after spending a month at Pannaway House, a man named Christopher Levett presented a more realistic scene in a letter to his friends back home. He wrote,

*I will not tell you that you may smell the cornfields before you
can smell the land, neither must men think that corn doth
grow naturally (or on trees), nor will the deer come when they
are called or stand still and look on a man until he shoots him
. . . nor the fish leap into the kettle, nor on the dry land are they
so plentiful that you may dip them up in baskets . . . which is
no truer than that the fowles will present themselves to you
with spits through them.*

Of course, natural resources were plentiful when compared to England, where people had been clearing forests and taking game animals for centuries. Levett finished by saying, "But certainly, there is fowl, deer, and fish enough for the taking if men be diligent."

Although they felt far from civilization, the inhabitants of Pannaway House were not alone. They had friendly contact with the Abenaki. The Indians showed their new neighbors how to make maple syrup and grow local crops. It is also likely that the Indians taught the settlers skills to stay alive through the long, difficult winters.

In the mid-1620s, the second New Hampshire plantation began. Edward Hilton, a fishmonger who lived in London, decided to seek his fortune in Piscataqua. He and his brother moved to Great Island, in the harbor at the mouth of the Piscataqua River, and set up a fish-drying operation. Soon after, they teamed up with several of the Pannaway House settlers and moved about 7 miles (11 km)

fishmonger—a merchant who specializes in selling fish

upriver. They built houses, planted corn, and traded with Indians in nearby villages. The new settlement became known as Hilton's Point.

THE LACONIA COMPANY

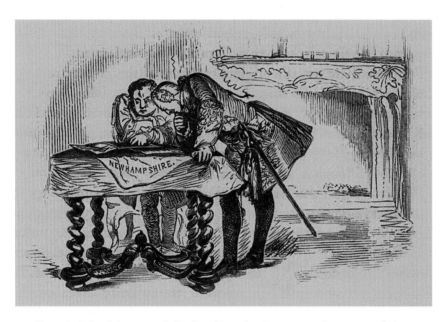

Captain John Mason and Sir Ferdinando Gorges study a map of their 1622 land grant in New England.

Captain John Mason, an English explorer and mapmaker, had spent six years (1615–1621) as the governor of the English colony at Newfoundland. In 1622, his friend Sir Ferdinando Gorges arranged for the two of them to share a large patent encompassing land that included present-day Maine and New Hampshire. Gorges and Mason split their patent between them, with Mason getting all the land between the Merrimack and Piscataqua Rivers. Mason, who was from the English county of Hampshire, decided to call the region New Hampshire. The Council for New England awarded Mason a charter for the newly formed Laconia Company, which he intended to use to develop his land.

The Laconia Company's goal was to control the fur trade in the area by locating and controlling the Lake of the Iroquois, rumored to be a huge lake teeming with beavers and other animals whose pelts were highly valued back in Europe. Mason, who remained in England, outfitted an expedition headed by Walter Neale, a former English soldier. From 1629 to 1631, 66 men and 22 women traveled to the Piscataqua region as part of the Laconia Company. They started fishing, producing lumber, and making salt from seawater, to ship back to England at a profit. They also brought seeds for planting grain and grapes, as well as blankets, liquor, cloth, and kettles to trade with the Indians. Neale set up his headquarters in Pannaway House, which the Laconia Company leased.

Walter Neale set out several times to find Lake of the Iroquois. He got as far as the White Mountains but found no lake. The shortage of furs in the area around Piscataqua forced the Laconia Company into bankruptcy before the end of 1634. The small plantations and farms established by the Laconia Company, however, survived. They became the first towns of New Hampshire.

LAKE *of the* IROQUOIS

EUROPEAN EXPLORERS HAD NO IDEA WHAT THEY MIGHT find in North America, and they sometimes believed in things that simply weren't there.

Native Americans often talked about very large bodies of water. Perhaps they were referring to Lake Winnipesauke (below), Lake Champlain, or even the Great Lakes. The enormous Lake of the Iroquois was supposed to be the source of all the rivers in New England as well as the St. Lawrence River in Canada and the Hudson River in New York. Many Europeans believed that this gigantic lake would be surrounded by countless miles of swamps, streams, and rivers, which would in turn provide an endless supply of beaver and other fur-bearing animals for the fur trade. The Europeans also reasoned that if all the major rivers came from a single source, whoever controlled this great body of water would control the continent's commerce, which depended on the rivers for transport. But the fabled Lake of the Iroquois was just a fantasy.

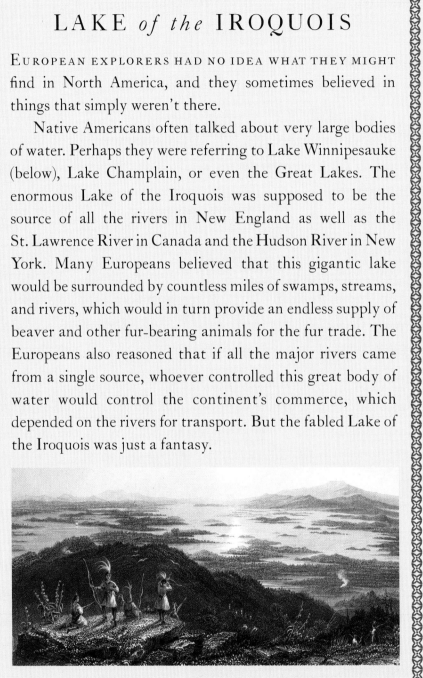

STRAWBERY BANKE

While Neale was setting up at Pannaway House, a man named Ambrose Gibbins took charge of the company's trading activities. He traveled upriver to a set of waterfalls that the Abenaki called Newichawannock. Today they're called Salmon Falls. The falls marked the point where saltwater no longer flowed upstream, and the Abenaki often gathered there to fish. Gibbins built a trading post there, but the trade didn't live up to his hopes. The Abenaki were more skilled at bargaining than Gibbins had expected.

In 1630, Captain Mason put Thomas Warnerton in charge of building a new, large plantation. Two miles (3 km) away from Pannaway House, Warnerton found a sunny clearing where a broad hill sloped up away from the river's edge. The hill was covered with strawberries, so the settlers called the place Strawbery Banke. They built what they would call the Great House. Larger and more elegant than Pannaway House, the Great House was surrounded by a deep ditch, like a moat, and a palisade wall. It had eight cannon inside. At the entrance to the harbor, the settlers also built a small fort and put four more cannon there.

Settlers continued to build small houses, storehouses, and shelters for the cows and sheep that had begun to arrive from Europe. The settlers dug wells, expanded the fish-drying platforms, and built a sawmill beside the river.

Mason, however, had no intention of creating a self-sufficient colony. He wanted the settlers to discover gold and find Lake of the Iroquois, and then rely on the profits that would come from the fur trade in that region. When his employees ran short on supplies, Mason simply sent more. He was often generous with what he sent, because he believed *"If there were once a discovery of the Lakes . . . I should, in some reasonable time, be reimbursed again."* But Mason's wealth was not without limits, and his investors had yet to see a return.

investor—one who supports a project with money in exchange for a portion of whatever profits are made

In 1633, Mason informed Neale that the money was running out. He ordered Neale to dismiss his household staff and return to England at once. He left a man named Godfrey in charge at Pannaway House, Warnerton in charge at Strawbery Banke, and Gibbins in charge at Newichawannock.

Later that year, the Laconia Company broke up and split its remaining assets among its owners. Gorges was given the

asset—anything of value

patent for Maine, including the islands off the coast of New Hampshire that are still part of Maine today. Mason received most of New Hampshire. He invested his remaining fortune in building a sawmill at the Newichawannock waterfalls. Strawbery Banke prospered under Warnerton's leadership. Wives of the men living there had begun to arrive from England in 1631. By 1640 there were 170 inhabitants in Strawbery Banke.

In December 1635, Captain John Mason died suddenly at the age of 49. With Pannaway House all but deserted, there were three plantations in the territory that passed to his heirs: the small settlement on Hilton's Point, which had continued to grow; Newichawannock, with its mill by the waterfall; and Strawbery Banke, which was growing into a town very different from the Puritan towns in neighboring Massachusetts.

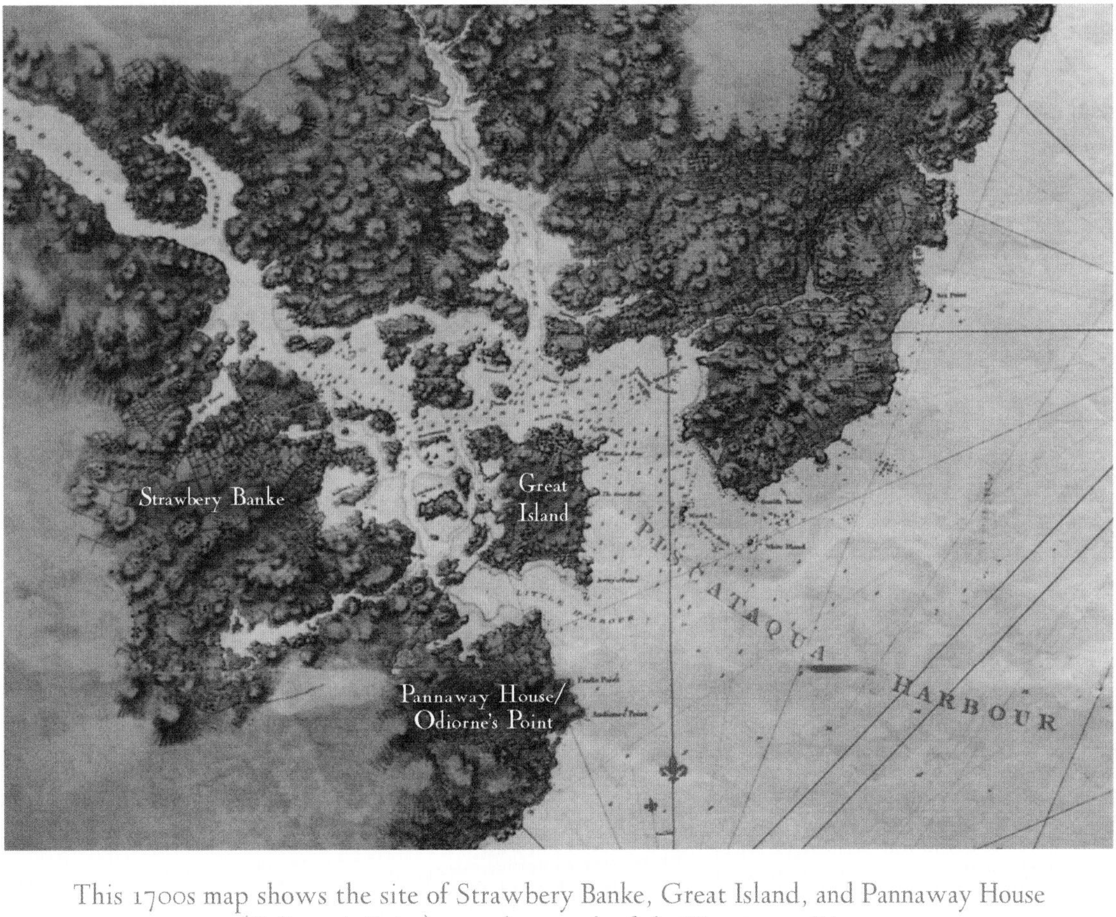

This 1700s map shows the site of Strawbery Banke, Great Island, and Pannaway House (Odiorne's Point) near the mouth of the Piscataqua River.

CHAPTER THREE

Massachusetts Gains Control

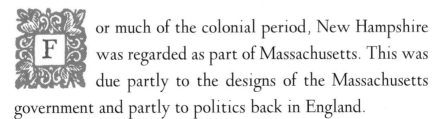

MASSACHUSETTS VIES FOR CONTROL *over New Hampshire*
as Puritan influence grows in the towns of
Dover and Exeter.

F or much of the colonial period, New Hampshire was regarded as part of Massachusetts. This was due partly to the designs of the Massachusetts government and partly to politics back in England.

New Hampshire and Massachusetts had very different origins. Puritans, a Protestant group at odds with the Church of England, had founded the Plymouth colony and the Massachusetts Bay colony in order to gain religious freedom. New Hampshire was about making money.

OPPOSITE: Settlers in the town of Dover labor to build homes for their families and shelter for their livestock in this wood engraving of life in New Hampshire in 1623.

Massachusetts settlers brought their families with them, while New Hampshire settlers were mostly young, single men searching for adventure and fortune. Often, the adventurers, trappers, traders, and sailors of New Hampshire ignored the church. Their Puritan neighbors greatly disapproved of this behavior.

First known as Piscataqua, for the river on its eastern shore, and then Strawbery Banke for the wild strawberries that grew there, Portsmouth became New Hampshire's chief port, with timber and fish its main exports.

IMMIGRATION TO NEW HAMPSHIRE

Migration from Massachusetts was one of the main sources of population growth in New Hampshire in the 17th century. By the end of 1640, more than half the residents in the New Hampshire settlements were former residents of

Massachusetts. Some thought they would have better opportunities to make money. Ironically, some came in search of religious freedom, refusing to worship under the strict demands of the Puritans. Most resented Massachusetts laws in which there was no separation of church and state. In Massachusetts, attending worship services was mandatory; the church dictated behavior and provided harsh punishments for the disobedient.

Most of the people who moved from Massachusetts to New Hampshire in search of more liberty came voluntarily. Others left Massachusetts in a hurry because they feared arrest by Puritan authorities. Piscataqua residents often protected the fugitives. One Massachusetts man complained that it was New Hampshire's *"usual manner to countenance . . . all such lewd persons as fled from us to them."*

PURITAN INFLUENCE

Some authorities in Massachusetts believed that the best way to deal with their New Hampshire neighbors was to find a way to exert legal control over New Hampshire itself. By the early 1630s, Massachusetts had begun establishing Puritan towns deep within New Hampshire territory. Another tactic was to claim that the Piscataqua land belonged to Massachusetts. This claim was based on the fact that charters that governed Massachusetts overlapped with New Hampshire's charters in several places.

Sometimes these two methods were used together. In 1632, the Puritans managed to convince the Hilton brothers that their ownership of Hilton's Point was very likely to be overturned. Afraid of losing everything, the Hiltons sold their rights to the land to a group of Puritan investors. Then the investors, at the direction of the authorities in Massachusetts, set up a Puritan town called Dover where Hilton's Point had been. They sent a man named Thomas Wiggin to be governor. Wiggin had a meetinghouse built and hired a Puritan minister named William Leveredge to conduct services there. New Hampshire settlers who preferred the Massachusetts way of governing moved to Dover. Puritan settlers from outside New Hampshire began to arrive as well.

A settler in a Puritan town is punished for his offense by being forced to endure public scorn while being confined in a wooden framework called a pillory. This punishment was common in New England in the 1600s.

Sometimes Puritan influence spread in New Hampshire even when Massachusetts did not intend it to. In 1637, a Puritan minister named John Wheelwright was banished from Massachusetts after defending his sister-in-law, Anne Hutchinson, who had been tried for heresy and banished. Wheelwright sailed north, looking for a spot to found his own Puritan community. He chose a site beside a water-fall on the Squamscott River. There were a few pioneering settlers there already, but Wheelwright convinced them to join him. Then, since the land did not seem to be covered by any patent or charter, he purchased it from the local Indians. He wrote a set of community reg-ulations and then sent for his family and other families he knew who were willing to follow him. Together, they founded and built the town of Exeter.

heresy—a religious opinion that contradicts the official opinion of a church

Although Exeter was a Puritan town and more similar to Massachusetts settlements than its neighboring town of Strawbery Banke, Massachusetts authorities were unhappy to have another town outside their control so close by. In response, they formally charged Wheelwright with "unneighborly conduct." Then, hoping to extend Massachusetts's influence into the area to counter Wheelwright, they gave permission to a Puritan minister named Stephen Batchellor to found a new town in an area called Winnacunnet. This was a very promising region with good farmland, which included several fields that the

Abenaki had already cleared. Batchellor set about building the town he would name Hampton, after his hometown in England. Soon there was a church, town buildings, and more than 60 families.

The Puritans

THE PURITANS, OF WHOM THE SETTLERS OF PLYMOUTH are probably the most famous example, were a group of men and women with strong religious convictions that were sometimes at odds with the Anglican Church (Church of England), the official religious establishment in England. They were distrustful of religious officials and believed that elaborate ceremonies distracted churchgoers from the proper worship of God. They wanted their religion to be "pure," which is why people started calling them Puritans. The Puritans did not believe in any separation between church and state, and they wanted to live where their church could share authority with the civil government. They believed that such a government would lead to a stable and prosperous society—the society they hoped to build in the New World.

It is often said that the Puritans came to North America in search of religious freedom. That's true, but also misleading. The Puritans did come to North America to be free to practice their own kind of Christianity. But they had no intention of allowing anyone else to follow any other religious beliefs. Their goal was to build a community centered on the Puritan church and its values. Once in Massachusetts, they did just that.

THE MASSACHUSETTS MODEL

By 1640, there were four major settlements in New Hampshire. Strawbery Banke, along with nearby Great Island and the site of Pannaway House; Dover, which had grown out of the Newichawannock trading post and Hilton's Point; Wheelwright's town of Exeter; and Batchellor's town of Hampton. There was still no formal "New Hampshire." Since the collapse of the Laconia Company and the death of John Mason, there had been very little direction from England as to who was in charge of these towns and how they should be governed. The Plymouth and Massachusetts Bay colonies were eager to extend Puritan influence over the region. Although many settlers in the Piscataqua region were determined to remain free of Puritan authority, many other people in New Hampshire wanted the advantages of being governed by Massachusetts.

Puritan towns in New Hampshire followed the Massachusetts model of holding town meetings to make decisions. At regular intervals, or as situations demanded, the residents of the town would meet to discuss and vote upon the business of the church and town. The town meetings also provided a place for residents to air their complaints. New Hampshire residents also looked to the Massachusetts court system for help. The Massachusetts General Court oversaw smaller, local, county courts. But, there was not yet any organized rule of law in New

Hampshire, and disagreements could be very difficult to resolve. Many New Hampshire residents believed that the Massachusetts General Court should extend its jurisdiction over the Piscataqua region by establishing a county court system there, too.

Towns built on the Massachusetts model tended to be well organized, prosperous, successful, and harmonious when compared to other towns of the time. Dover was the first town in New Hampshire to seek to place itself under Massachusetts's control. The authorities in Dover sent a petition, signed by many of the town's residents, to the Massachusetts General Court. The petition said that the inhabitants of Dover were complaining *"of the want of some good government amongst them and desired some help in this particular from . . . the Massachusetts Bay, whereby they may be ruled and ordered according unto God in both church and commonwealth."*

In 1641, the Massachusetts General Court granted the petition and extended its authority to all the territory west of the Piscataqua River except the town of Exeter. To reassure those in Dover who were not Puritans, Massachusetts made an exception for the town that allowed men who did not belong to the Puritan church to vote in town meetings. In 1643, Massachusetts took over Exeter as well, at the request of its citizens who had grown to dislike Wheelwright. Taking his most loyal followers, Wheelwright left Exeter to found a new town far to the north in what is now Maine.

Puritan minister John Wheelwright, banished from Massachusetts, founded the New Hampshire town of Exeter in 1638. When the town came under Massachusetts's control five years later, he moved to Maine and started a church in the town of Wells.

With Hampton, Dover, and Exeter all under Massachusetts control, only Strawbery Banke was left on its own. Late in 1643, the General Court declared its authority over the area, but the residents of Strawbery Banke seem to have ignored this action Instead, they continued to rely on the authority of Warnerton to settle local agreements between residents.

In the mid-1640s, Warnerton was killed in a drunken brawl at a French settlement far to the north while trying to sell off some of the Mason family's property. Henry Sherburne, another former Laconia employee, and John and Richard Cutt, who were area merchants, took over the government of Strawbery Banke.

THE MASON CLAIM

Around 1650, Joseph Mason sailed from England to America to inspect the Mason family's property there. Joseph Mason was a relative of Captain John Mason, acting on the orders of the captain's widow, Anne. There was not much Mason family property left in New Hampshire. A man named Richard Leader had taken over the sawmill at Newichawannock and refused to recognize John Mason's claim. Cattle and other trade goods had all been stolen or sold long ago. Former tenants of Mason had either left or, declaring that the Masons did not own the land anymore, taken ownership for themselves. Most of the buildings had been dismantled. Joseph Mason wrote that there was *"nothing left but the bare lands and the monuments of ruin."* He decided to sue to get his family's property back. He asked the Massachusetts General Court to review his claim.

tenant—one who pays rent for the right to live on another's property

The General Court decided that Richard Leader had seized the Newichawannock sawmill illegally and ordered him to return it to the Mason family. That decision worried the men who had become leaders of Strawbery Banke. They all owned property that the Mason family claimed. If the General Court made other decisions in the Mason family's favor, they stood to lose everything. In October 1651, they took action to keep that from happening. They drew up a petition that asked the General Court to recognize their titles of ownership, to establish a town at Strawbery Banke, and to set up a local court. The petition said that if Massachusetts was willing to take such action, it could have authority over the area. Since Massachusetts wanted to have its authority recognized in Strawbery Banke and to set up a court there, it decided to grant the petition. It passed a law that any title that had been in place at least five years was valid, even if it conflicted with the Mason family's claims. And it declared that Strawbery Banke, Great Island, and the surrounding area were now parts of a town called Portsmouth.

petition—a formal written request

By 1652, all of the towns in New Hampshire were entirely under the control of Massachusetts.

H:Lords:

Chara Deum soboles:

Magnu Iovis Incrementum.

York

D: Gloc:

H:Comons

Bishops & the Comoh prafer Booke

Traytors rewarded:

Sectaries reiected:

CHAPTER FOUR

Royal New Hampshire

MASSACHUSETTS LOSES ITS CLAIMS *to the New Hampshire settlements as the Nichols Commission defines the borders. In 1680, New Hampshire becomes a royal colony, overseen by the Lords of Trade.*

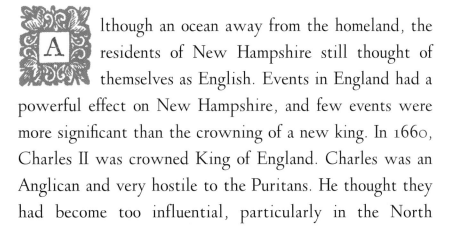lthough an ocean away from the homeland, the residents of New Hampshire still thought of themselves as English. Events in England had a powerful effect on New Hampshire, and few events were more significant than the crowning of a new king. In 1660, Charles II was crowned King of England. Charles was an Anglican and very hostile to the Puritans. He thought they had become too influential, particularly in the North

OPPOSITE: A 1660 engraving illustrates King Charles II presiding over the two branches of Parliament. Beneath them are bishops with the Church of England's Common Prayer book, and in the bottom frames traitors are being punished while heretics are expelled from the country.

American colonies. For people in New Hampshire who did not agree with the Massachusetts Puritans, this was very good news indeed. One of those people was Robert Tufton Mason. He was Captain John Mason's grandson, and he had inherited all John Mason's claims in New Hampshire. He petitioned Parliament to look into Massachusetts's conduct in New Hampshire.

Parliament—Britain's lawmaking body

THE NICHOLS COMMISSION

Parliament created a commission, headed by a friend of Masons named Colonel Richard Nichols, to travel to New England to review the matter. Arriving in July 1664, the members of the commission almost immediately decided that Massachusetts had assumed authority over territory that had never been legally granted to it by the Crown.

One of the commission's first public acts was to issue a correction regarding the Massachusetts border. According to its charter, the colony's northern border was an east/west line 3 miles (4.8 km) north of the Merrimack River. Massachusetts interpreted that to mean three miles north of the river's *source* at Lake Winnepesauke. The Nichols Commission declared that the border was actually three miles north of the river's *mouth*, that is, three miles north of the coast. Besides making Massachusetts significantly smaller, putting the border there meant that the New Hampshire settlements were definitely outside Massachusetts, thwarting Massachusetts's attempts to claim that its charter gave it authority over New Hampshire.

Next, the members of the Nichols Commission began trying to convince people to accept their authority, both as representatives of the king and as agents of the Mason family. They held hearings at Hampton, Dover, and Exeter and quickly learned that these towns had very strong ties to Massachusetts. Only the residents of Portsmouth seemed to genuinely welcome the Nichols Commission and the idea

People in New Hampshire gathered at meeting houses to discuss town business much like the New England colonists pictured in this 19th–century engraving.

of limiting Massachusetts's authority. Even there, the town leaders had been appointed or supported by Massachusetts. When Nichols told the Portsmouth residents at a public meeting that they were independent of Massachusetts, the leaders of Portsmouth wrote to the governor of Massachusetts, Richard Bellingham, asking him what they should do. They closed the letter with *"Haste! Post Haste!"* which meant they wanted a reply very quickly.

When the Nichols Commission held a similar meeting in Dover, there was more trouble. The Dover town meeting argued against accepting the commission's authority.

Nichols and his colleagues also encouraged residents who were unhappy with Massachusetts's rule to collect signatures on petitions for the commission to take back to England. A petition signed by Portsmouth residents complained that the leaders of Portsmouth had used religious discrimination to keep themselves in power. The petition claimed that Anglicans were never made freemen, so they could not vote, and were denied the right to worship and the right to Christian burial. The Portsmouth residents also claimed that all town offices and grants of town land were given only to Puritans.

The commission returned to England with its report, and Massachusetts sent an agent to England with a report and petitions of its own, declaring the colony's loyalty to the king and blaming all the trouble on the behavior of the Nichols Commission. Nothing ever came of either of these reports, however. It was clear, however, that Massachusetts's rule over New Hampshire was not secure.

THE LORDS OF TRADE

In order to secure control over the region, Massachusetts tried to purchase the patents of Maine and New Hampshire outright in 1672. King Charles did not want the Puritans to gain more power. He ordered the owners (including Robert Tufton Mason) not to sell the patents to Massachusetts. In 1674, King Charles created a new committee and gave it full control over New England's affairs. Called the Committee on Trade and Plantations, it was a part of the King's Privy Council, which meant that the king had direct control over the committee. Its members were known as the Lords of Trade. The Lords of Trade immediately announced an investigation of the situation in New England.

Mason arranged for a cousin, Edward Randolph, to become a member of the new committee and act as his agent. This time he promised to pay Randolph a percentage of any money he made on his family's New Hampshire patents. Randolph went to New Hampshire, but he was not gone long. In the years since the Nichols Commission, Massachusetts had tightened its control over the region, but Randolph found very few people complaining. This was partly because it had been more than 20 years since Massachusetts had taken over, and people were getting used to the colony's rule. Many of the people who had supported the Nichols Commission had either died or left. Besides, the truth was that Massachusetts was doing a good job of running New Hampshire.

When Randolph returned to England in the fall of 1676, he told Mason that they could count on very little support from people in New Hampshire. As a result, the Lords of Trade refused to take any real action against Massachusetts. They did, however, call for several changes in the way Massachusetts governed, reorganizing the government and sending in a governor appointed by the king.

MASSACHUSETTS
LOSES CONTROL

In 1679, the Lords of Trade, eager to enforce their recommendations in Massachusetts, decided to open an investigation into whether the colony should be allowed to keep its own charter, let alone control New Hampshire. In May 1679, Massachusetts was formally ordered to withdraw all its officers and agents from Portsmouth, Dover, Exeter, and Hampton. Mason was given some of what he wanted. He would own all unowned land within his patent and have the right to collect money from people who had settled on the lands covered by his patent. He would not be allowed to collect back rent, nor would he have any governing authority over New Hampshire. To govern in New Hampshire, the Lords of Trade decided to set up a Provincial Council made up of royal appointees, and an assembly, whose members would be elected by the freemen at their town meetings. The president of the council would serve as governor. The Lords of Trade decided to offer positions on the council to the men who were already in charge. John Cutt, an official at Strawbery Banke, was offered the presidency.

On January 1, 1680, New Hampshire became a royal colony under the direct authority of King Charles. How obedient the colonists would be remained to be seen. ❧

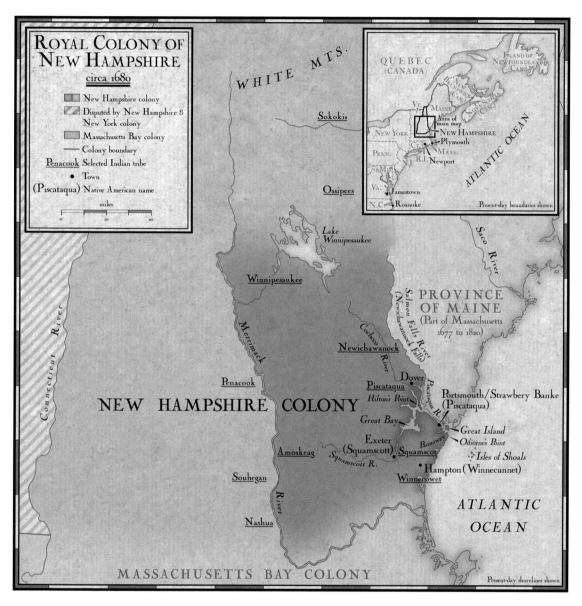

ROYAL COLONY OF NEW HAMPSHIRE
circa 1680

- New Hampshire colony
- Disputed by New Hampshire & New York colony
- Massachusetts Bay colony
- —— Colony boundary
- Penacook Selected Indian tribe
- • Town
- (Piscataqua) Native American name

miles
0   10   20

QUEBEC (CANADA)

ISLAND OF NEWFOUNDLAND (CAN.)

Area of main map

NEW HAMPSHIRE

Plymouth

MASS.

Newport

R.I.

CT.

N.J.

MD.

VA.

Jamestown

N.C.

Roanoke

NEW YORK

PENN.

MAINE

Vt.

ATLANTIC OCEAN

Present-day boundaries shown

WHITE MTS.

Sokokis

Ossipees

Lake Winnipesaukee

Saco River

PROVINCE OF MAINE
(Part of Massachusetts 1677 to 1820)

Winnipesaukee

Merrimack River

Connecticut River

Cochecho River

Salmon Falls River (Newichawannock Falls)

Newichawanock

Penacook

NEW HAMPSHIRE COLONY

Dover

Piscataqua
Hilton's Point

Piscataqua R.

Portsmouth/Strawbery Banke (Piscataqua)

Great Bay

Great Island
Odiorne's Point

Exeter (Squamscott)

Squamscot

Pannaway

Isles of Shoals

Amoskeag

Squamscott R.

Souhegan

Hampton (Winnecunnet)

Winnecowet

Nashua

River

ATLANTIC OCEAN

MASSACHUSETTS BAY COLONY

Present-day shorelines shown

The boundaries of the Royal Colony of New Hampshire were not clearly defined in 1680. There were only four towns—Portsmouth, Dover, Exeter, and Hampton—all of which were founded in the region explored by Martin Pring in 1603 (dark red on map). Although New Hampshire's Algonquian people were collectively known as Abenaki, individual tribes had their own names. This map shows where some of these groups lived.

CHAPTER FIVE

Life in New Hampshire

FARMING, LOGGING, AND MASTING *become important businesses in the colony, spurring more people to move to New Hampshire. Violence with Native Americans results as settlers push the Abenaki off their land.*

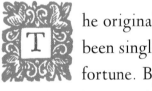he original New Hampshire settlers had mostly been single men looking for a way to make their fortune. By the 18th century, more women had arrived, and most colonists lived as families.

The husband was considered the head of a family. The wife was not considered equal to her husband. Although women managed the family and the household and in rare cases helped out with the family business, they sat separately

OPPOSITE: New Hampshire colonists walk through a meadow while cows graze in the background in this landscape by artist, Samuel Colman. Many colonists took to farming land outside of town where there was more space for planting and for livestock.

in church and were not allowed to vote or hold office. A man in New Hampshire summed up the place of women at the time in a short poem:

Small is the province of a wife,
And narrow is her sphere in life,
Within that sphere to move aright,
Should be her principal delight.

Most families had at least four children, partly because there was so much work to be done. Daughters were expected to serve their parents' household until they married, and sons were expected to work for their fathers until they turned 21. Children were also expected to care for their parents when they were too old to care for themselves. Like today, however, young people did not always do what was expected of them. One man wrote in 1757, *"Young people grow uncommonly loose, rude, vain, and ungoverned, and if restrained by their superiors immediately . . . get clear of their parents."*

FARMING

Throughout the colonial world, nearly everybody was a farmer. An average family raised almost all the food it ate. Most people also raised produce or livestock to sell for a profit, and it was common to trade produce for things that skilled craftspeople made.

Fences were essential, and several towns created officers whose job was to oversee their maintenance. *"Every man must secure his corn and meadow against great cattle,"* ran one order of 1642, *"and if any damage be done by such cattle, it shall be borne by him through whose insufficient fence the cattle did enter."*

Early on, farming was mostly cooperative. In cooperative farming, the town would set aside land near the center of the settlement for everyone to share. Everyone helped with the planting and harvesting. The town made sure that enough seed was saved for the next year's planting, and any surplus produce was distributed to those in need. There was also public land for grazing livestock. The livestock bore two brands: one identifying the town and the other identifying the owner.

A young girl tends her family's cows, making sure they make their way home from their grazing land back to the barn for the night.

As time passed, individual farms became more common. Increasing populations meant that there were more and more people who wanted to farm on the same town land. Since the town farmland was usually surrounded by buildings, it was difficult to expand. Families began clearing new fields outside the town proper. Eventually, the public land in the towns was needed for other things, and cooperative farming disappeared. But the tradition of helping each other at harvest or with other tasks continued.

MILLS

By the late 1600s, colonists were using water-powered mills to produce flour and lumber. People usually grew their own grain, but grinding the grain into flour took a great deal of time and work. Mills for grinding grain into flour were called gristmills. The river turned waterwheels that, in turn, rotated huge, round stones inside the mill. One stone was placed on top of another, and they would grind grain that was placed between them. For payment, the miller usually took a portion of the flour that was produced.

The forests of New Hampshire were one of its most attractive natural resources, as far as the rest of the world was concerned. In Europe, and England in particular, much of the available wood had been cut down long ago. Lumber mills, also called sawmills, turned logs cut from New Hampshire's large forests into planks and boards for building. Cutting timber into boards by hand was very time-consuming, so it was easier for people to buy what they needed from a mill. The waterwheel in a sawmill powered saws that cut the logs into boards and planks that were usually more even and uniform than the handmade variety. Sawmills could produce more lumber than was needed for building within a town. This meant that the surplus could be used for trading with other towns and colonies and even with England. New Hampshire residents exported shingles, barrels, and planks and boards of many shapes and sizes. The town of Dover had half a dozen sawmills in operation within a generation of its founding.

Loggers chop and fell a pine tree in one of New Hampshire's plentiful forests during a snowy winter. The log will be dragged by a team of oxen to the nearest swift waterway, which will carry it downstream to a sawmill.

MASTING AND NAVAL STORES

Trees that had been milled into masts for sailing ships became one of New Hampshire's most valuable exports. The masts of 17th- and 18th-century sailing ships had to be made from a single tall tree trunk in order to be strong enough to carry the sails. New Hampshire white pine was ideal, because the ancient trees were huge by European standards, and they could withstand ocean storms and winds. Masting was dangerous but highly profitable work. Masting crews consisting of 20 or 30 men traveled far into the forest looking for suitable trees. When they found one, it was cut down and then moved with the help of many men and teams of oxen to the nearest swift river. Then it was floated down to Portsmouth.

Naval stores and shipbuilding became major New Hampshire industries. By the middle of the 17th century, ships were being built in Portsmouth, and ship parts such as rope and specialized lumber were being sent for sale to shipyards in England.

Naval stores—tar, hemp, and other goods needed to build ships

By the 1660s, trading companies in England had begun to notice that New Hampshire, which they had considered an isolated, unimportant colony, was producing very high-quality goods for shipbuilding. One company sent a representative named William Vaughn to evaluate the situation. He was so impressed that he quit his job, stayed in New Hampshire, and became one of Portsmouth's most successful merchants. Even today, the shipyards at Portsmouth are among the most respected in the world, producing everything from small boats to huge warships for the U.S. Navy.

CONFLICT WITH THE ABENAKI

The decades surrounding the turn of the 18th century were difficult for New Hampshire colonists and Native Americans alike. European settlers took over more and more of the Indians' lands, crowding the tribes and infringing upon their hunting and farming areas. New Hampshire towns continued to grow, pushing the Abenaki farther and farther out. Several accounts describe the deterioration of tribal life. As early as 1642, a Narragansett chief complained, *"You know our fathers had plenty of deer . . . and our coves were full of fish and fowl. But these English have gotten our land, they with scythes cut down the grass, and with axes fell the trees; their cows and horses eat the grass, and their hogs spoil our clam Bankes, and we shall be starved."* And as late as 1789, a Mohegan remembered better times before the Europeans: *"The times are Exceedingly Altered, Yea the times have turn'd everything upside down. . . .Chiefly by the help of the White People, for in times past, our Fore-Fathers . . . had everything in great plenty. . . .But alas, it is not so now, all our Fishing, Hunting and Fowling is entirely gone."*

Harsh weather, disease, and famine took their toll on everyone. A New Hampshire merchant named Samuel Lane kept a particularly detailed record:

1748—We had a tedious hard cold and most difficult winter, by reason of [as] much snow & bad passing, 'tis said, ever known by any person now living. The cold began severe about ye 27th of November & held constant 26 days. On ye 3rd of December, the deep snow began to come, and held near 4 months, so exceeding deep that there was scarcely any passing in roads. I counted 25 snows . . . in all, they contained about 12 feet in depth. This is the second hard winter together.

We had a terrible drought in the Summer, which cut short our . . . corn and grass very much. Much damage done by fires in the woods.

1749—Most disturbing drought . . . people strive to keep their cattle alive; many go 40, 50, or 60 miles into the woods to cut meadows. . . . Some cut leaves off trees & carry them into their barns, etc. for cattle to live on.

As land and resources became scarce, conflict with the colonists became inevitable. Gradually, the friendship that had been traditional between the Abenaki and the New Hampshire settlers faded into memory.

These conflicts were often encouraged by European nations. A common European strategy of the time was to urge the Indian population of a region to attack and drive out the settlers of a rival country's colony. In what is now Canada, to the north of New Hampshire, the French enjoyed good relations with the Native Americans because the French maintained only small trading outposts rather than growing communities. To drive out the English, French traders encouraged the Abenaki to make war on the New Hampshire settlers. In 1689 and 1690, there was a series of bloody raids on settlements just up the river from the Newichawannock Falls, where decades earlier the first contact between the English and the Abenaki had taken place. In the summer of 1690, 30 settlers and an unknown number of Indians were killed in fighting in and around the town of Dover. Between 1692 and 1696, Portsmouth was raided four times, each time with heavy casualties.

New Hampshire colonists are attacked on the river by Indians angry with the loss of their lands and way of life.

As the raids became more frequent, the English began to be more aggressive about hunting down and attacking the Indians. Tribal villages were destroyed, crops were burned, and captives were sold into slavery. There is no record of exactly what happened to the New Hampshire Abenaki. Most likely they moved farther north, where fewer English had settled, and Algonquian tribes were friendly. By 1730, most of the Abenaki had left New Hampshire.

GROWTH SLOWS

Although New Hampshire ultimately survived, decades of fighting had a profound effect on the colony. For one thing, a large portion of the towns' resources had to be devoted to organized defenses. Small forts called garrison houses were built and maintained at the public expense. Arms and ammunition were bought in large amounts. Lane mentioned these defenses several times in his journal:

> 1743—*Indians troublesome this year. People kept garrison at Newmarket.*

> 1744—*Many people driven out of the woods by Indians and people kept garrison at Newmarket; Alarms made often. Where I live, we heard alarms often & horns sounded . . . and people much distressed by the Indians.*

The diary of a minister named John Pike, who lived in Dover, also records the events of this dangerous time:

John Church, sen. [Senior], slain by the Indians as he travelled to seek his horse . . .

Joseph Pittman slain by the Indians as he was guarding some mowers not far from the Oyster River meeting house . . .

Maturin Ricker killed in his field and his little son carried away.

Even though the English population of New Hampshire had been increasing steadily, the years of warfare brought this growth almost to a halt. Small settlements far from the protection of larger towns were abandoned as settlers moved to the towns for safety. Besides the deaths of colonists, buildings, crops, and livestock were destroyed, and food shortages became common. In 1752, Samuel Lane wrote in his diary: *"such a scarcity of provisions both corn & meat that it [would] make almost the hardest heart ache, to hear the complaints of multitudes of people, ready to famish for want of food, begging for a handful of corn."* In 1713 European nations signed a peace treaty called the Treaty of Utrecht. Among other things, this meant that European countries stopped trying to encourage war in the colonies between settler and native. Very slowly, this peace took hold in the colonies. Unfortunately, by this time, British settlers had become so aggressive about driving away the Native Americans that one New Hampshire man wrote, *"There are no Indians in this province that we know of."* With the fighting over, however, there was time for New Hampshire to heal and grow.

CHAPTER SIX

Life Under the Lords of Trade

ROYAL GOVERNOR EDWARD CRANFIELD *enforces the Navigation Acts until the Lords of Trade bow to pressure and remove him. New Hampshire becomes part of the Dominion of New England.*

B y 1681, the Lords of Trade had begun to realize that it had been a mistake to put John Cutt and his friends in charge of New Hampshire. Right from the start, Cutt and his allies had made it clear that their loyalty still lay with Massachusetts. There were particular problems surrounding a set of laws called the Navigation

OPPOSITE: English galleons like this one were used were used to stop and seize ships carrying cargo that was not in compliance with the Navigation Acts.

Acts, passed by Parliament between 1651 and 1660. The Navigation Acts were supposed to govern trade in and with the American colonies. The laws were unpopular in most of the Colonies because they limited trade to England and placed regulations on what could be imported to the Colonies from Asia and Africa. New Hampshire residents had found a way around the Navigation Acts: smuggling. Portsmouth was a thriving seaport town, and many of its leaders, as well as those in other parts of the colony, were successful smugglers themselves. They had never enforced the Navigation Acts.

The harbor at Portsmouth, New Hampshire, as seen from the shore in 1777

To ensure that the Navigation Acts were enforced, Edward Randolph, who had investigated the Mason claims in New Hampshire in 1675, was sent back to America and put in charge of customs. His assistant was

Walter Barefoote. Cutt and the others colonial leaders refused to cooperate with the trade regulations. When Randolph seized ships and cargoes that were in violation of the law, Cutt encouraged the shipowners to sue Randolph. Since the court officials favored the colonists, Randolph was certain to lose. When Randolph ordered Barefoote to open a customs office in Portsmouth, Cutt ordered him not to. When Barefoote disobeyed Cutt and opened the office anyway, Cutt had him arrested. He was fined, not only for his disobedience, but also because throughout the entire trial the only thing he would say, over and over, was "*My name is Walter.*"

The conflict reached a peak when an assistant of Barefoote's tried to search a ship that belonged to one of Cutt's councilors, William Vaughn. Vaughn beat the customs official so seriously with his cane that it took the man several months to recover.

After another investigation, the Lords of Trade decided on a new plan. In 1682, they sent an army officer named Edward Cranfield to be the new governor of New Hampshire. The new governor's powers were considerable. He was to seek the advice of the council and the assembly, but he was under no obligation to follow their advice. He could veto any law he didn't approve of. He could remove and replace any council or assembly member he didn't like. And he could remove and appoint judges and court officers as he saw fit.

veto—the power to overturn a decision

The Navigation Acts

THE REGULATION OF TRADE WAS VITAL IF ENGLAND WAS TO realize any benefits from its colonial holdings. In the middle of the 17th century, Parliament passed a variety of laws governing all aspects of trade by ships in the Colonies. These were called the Navigation Acts.

From the perspective of most colonists, these laws were at best a nuisance and at worst unfair. Most were designed to benefit England, rather than the Colonies or the colonists. The justification was that since the Colonies were part of England, any benefit to England would ultimately benefit the English in America as well.

Distance from England made the enforcement of the Navigation Acts very difficult, and in many American ports they were all but ignored. This was particularly true of Portsmouth, which had a reputation for smuggling, and which petitioned Parliament several times to be made exempt from the Navigation Acts. Any leader of New Hampshire appointed or supported by the Crown was immediately faced with the nearly impossible task of enforcing the acts. This led directly to the downfall of several of them. Where the Navigation Acts were enforced, they caused friction and sometimes violence. Discontent over the Navigation Acts was ultimately one of the causes leading to the American Revolution.

Edward Cranfield intended to take complete control. He forced through a law that let sheriffs choose who would sit on juries in the courts. Since Cranfield was responsible for choosing the sheriffs, he now had control of judges, sheriffs, and juries.

Cranfield also passed several strict laws regarding trade. Not only did these laws help to enforce the Navigation Acts, they were also designed to personally hurt his opponents. For example, he made it very difficult for New Hampshire residents to get permission to trade with any other New England colony, especially Massachusetts. Most of the former councilors were Puritan merchants with extensive ties to Massachusetts. Finally, Cranfield acted to limit the power and influence of the Puritans in New Hampshire. In 1683 he passed laws that ordered Puritan ministers to give baptism and church membership to anyone that the Anglican Church would have admitted.

As Cranfield passed stricter and stricter laws, the residents of New Hampshire resisted. They also complained to the Lords of Trade. Finally Cranfield himself wrote to the Lords of Trade, begging for a new assignment far away from New Hampshire. When his request was granted and he was sent to Barbados in 1685, he wrote, "I esteem it the greatest happiness that ever I had in my life that your Lordships have given me an opportunity to remove from these unreasonable people. . . . No man shall be acceptable to them that puts his Majesty's commands in execution."

John Cutt

John Cutt was born in England in 1625. Sometime before 1645, he immigrated to the American colonies with his brothers, Richard and Robert. They began a small fishing and trading operation on the Isles of Shoals. They soon moved their business to the mainland, setting up trade in Strawbery Banke (which would later become Portsmouth). They exported lumber, naval stores, and fish, and they owned several mills.

John Cutt served as selectman for Portsmouth for many years. His power was considerable. A local tavern owner complained that Cutt and others *"ruled, swayed and ordered all offices, both civil and military, at their pleasure."*

A Puritan, Cutt got along well with Massachusetts authorities. Nevertheless, when New Hampshire was made a royal colony in 1680, it was Cutt who was named president of the Provincial Council.

At age 54, President Cutt was already considered *"ancient and infirm."* Indeed, his rival for the post, Richard Waldron, agreed to support Cutt's appointment only if he himself was made deputy, on the assumption that Cutt would die soon after taking office. Early in 1681, Cutt became ill. He died in late March of that year.

DOMINION OF NEW ENGLAND

For more than a year there was no official word from England on how New Hampshire should be governed. Although there was no one actually in charge of the colony, the colonists got on with their day-to-day life, and there were only minor problems. The town meetings were especially helpful in settling small disputes that arose over property boundaries, deeds, and business transactions. Even those who had never supported the Massachusetts faction began to see the value of the town meeting system.

In 1685, King Charles II died, and his brother, the Duke of York, was crowned King James II. King James was very unpopular, mostly because of his religious beliefs. King James was Catholic, and most English people were Anglicans (Protestants). James hated the idea of elected assemblies, town meetings, and self-government. The king encouraged the Lords of Trade to finally revoke the charter of the Massachusetts Bay Colony.

King James II of England

This decision worried many people in New Hampshire who still thought of themselves as part of Massachusetts. But the last two years had shown that the colony could get by without any one person actually running things. Many people in New Hampshire must have begun to realize how independent they had already become, without actually trying.

King James decided that his royal colonies would be governed under the same system that the Spanish used in their colonies. A viceroy would be appointed, who would oversee everything in the king's name. Governors, councils, judges, and other officials would be appointed directly by the king or his representatives. James decided to lump the various colonies of New England together into one big colony called the Dominion of New England.

viceroy—one who represents and acts in the name of a king or queen

Under the Dominion of New England, New Hampshire was not a separate entity with its own rulers. Instead, the dominion's capital was established in Boston. Men who had been given positions of authority in New Hampshire all left for the new capital city. The Massachusetts Puritans immediately began causing trouble for the new dominion authorities. This was to New Hampshire's advantage. No one in charge in the dominion had time to worry about four towns up in the northern pine forests. New Hampshire was more or less left alone.

A set of playing cards celebrating the 1688 Glorious Revolution in England displays anti-Catholic drawings expressing the English peoples' dislike of King James II.

THE GLORIOUS REVOLUTION

In 1688, King James II was overthrown in a revolution without any bloodshed. It became known as the Glorious Revolution. His daughter, Queen Mary II, and her Dutch husband, William of Orange, who became King William III in England, reestablished Protestant rule. James II fled to France. When word of this overthrow reached New England, Puritans in Massachusetts arrested all the dominion officials. The new king and queen sent a proclamation to New England ordering that those leaders who had been in charge since the arrest of the dominion officials should stay in charge until further notice.

This order created an interesting situation for Portsmouth, Dover, Exeter, and Hampton. Massachusetts had gone back to governing under its old charter, but New Hampshire had been a royal colony before King James created the Dominion of New England, and William and Mary sent no new specific instructions. New Hampshire again found itself without government, and this time, there was some question whether New Hampshire even existed as a separate colony. No valid document said that it did. The four towns decided to petition Massachusetts to take control. In 1690, New Hampshire again came under Massachusetts's authority. Massachusetts hoped that this time the arrangement would be permanent.

ROYAL AGAIN

In the early 1690s, an energetic businessman named Samuel Allen decided to invest heavily in the New Hampshire region. He bought out the Mason family and secured a large contract with the English Navy to supply masts and other naval stores. He then tried to convince the Lords of Trade and the new king to declare him governor of New Hampshire. When Massachusetts was issued a new charter in 1691, it specifically excluded Portsmouth, Dover, Hampton, and Exeter. In 1692, Allen was made governor of the royal colony of New Hampshire. New Hampshire would remain a royal colony until it finally became independent during the American Revolution. ✹

CHAPTER SEVEN

A Time of Growth

New Hampshire successfully operates *under local leadership, but shares a governor with Massachusetts until 1740, when Benning Wentworth becomes governor of the colony.*

I n the early 18th century, as the hostility with the Native Americans finally subsided, another long-standing problem was also put to rest: the issue of Massachusetts and its relationship to New Hampshire. When Governor Allen took over in the early 1690s, he quickly recognized the continuing conflict between those who believed New Hampshire should be independent of Massachusetts and those who did not.

opposite: Eleazar Wheelock oversees a group of young people reading aloud at a 1770 ceremony celebrating the founding of Dartmouth College in New Hampshire.

The Lords of Trade finally came up with a compromise. They appointed Lord Bellomont to replace Allen as governor of New Hampshire. At the same time, they made Bellomont governor of Massachusetts. While New Hampshire and Massachusetts were ordered to remain separate in all other things, a single man was put in charge of both. When immediate cooperation was needed for something such as organized defense, a single governor ensured that decisions would be made quickly. At the same time, New Hampshire was free to have its own leadership. The Massachusetts Puritans were also free to govern as they saw fit, but their authority would be limited to Massachusetts.

LOCAL RULE

The real business of running New Hampshire fell to the local authorities. Immediately under the governor, who was appointed by the Crown, was a lieutenant governor who would be in charge locally while the governor was elsewhere. Under the lieutenant governor, there was a council. The council members, leaders in the New Hampshire community, were appointed by the governor. To balance the appointed council, there was an assembly, sometimes called the House of Representatives, whose members were elected by the freemen in the towns. Its main power was the right to decide how money in the towns should be spent.

Below the assembly were the town meetings. Samuel Lane often recorded town meetings in his diary. In March 1744, he wrote, *"Town Meeting Day. I was chose Tything man."* (The tything man was a town officer in charge of, among other things, keeping the peace, enforcing the laws of the Sabbath, and recording those not present at church.) Attending the town meetings was not just the responsibility of prosperous merchants like Lane. Abner Sanger, a laborer of modest means, also kept a journal in which he recorded that he or his twin brother, El, attended the meetings. On February 12, 1775, Abner wrote, *"El to town meeting for choosing a deputy. Stormy night,"* and he noted on March 7, *"This is Town Meeting Day."* "Town Meeting Day" probably referred to the annual meeting, at which town officers were elected.

These meetings could carry the full force of law, and not everyone was happy with such power in the hands of the people. Town meetings could be a distressing prospect for someone who had gotten into some kind of trouble. This was particularly true for Tories, or those suspected of being Tories by the Whigs. On December 18, 1775, when El Sanger was suspected of being a Tory and hauled off to a meeting, Abner recorded the event along with a weather report: *"Fair northwest winds, but comfortable. El has to go off with a small mob to the committee at Keene town. I chop wood fit to sled.*

Tory—a colonist who remained loyal to Britain; also known as a Loyalist

Whig—a colonist who no longer supported the Crown

Grows cold." In fact, as this diary entry suggests, popular rule sometimes descended into mob rule. As early as December 1774, Sanger wrote, "*I go up to Mr. Carpenter's to see if or when they would help me sled wood. Dr. Blake there. They tell of mob come to Keene to visit tories. Also they tell of near all the people in Two-Penny Parish is gone to see the mob.*" And things were little different the following May: "*I go up to Captain Dorman's in morning. I drive p[l]ow for him in the meadow. Warm. Afternoon a mob comes and takes care of the tories in Keene. . . . We plow until near dark then go up and find the mob has not done with the tories. They spend until midnight.*" Samuel Lane was more explicit in his contempt for popular rule. He wrote: "*The course of Law and Courts of Justice are stop'd and almost all publick affairs are carried on and transacted by congresses & committees throu' most of this continent.*"

Despite occasional discontent and the danger of mob rule, the system worked well. The peaceful times, coupled with effective government, led to growth and prosperity for New Hampshire. The population began to soar, thanks to more children being born and immigration into the colony. There was a great deal of migration north from colonies such as Massachusetts, Connecticut, and Rhode Island, which were also experiencing periods of growth.

Many other immigrants were British sailors and soldiers who deserted their ships to stay in New Hampshire. Most of the immigrants came from Ulster, a part of northern Ireland that had been settled by people of Scottish descent. New towns like Londonderry became outposts of

Scotch-Irish culture. These immigrants farmed potatoes and planted flax, which was made into thread that was woven into fine linen cloth. By 1730, more than a thousand people had come to New Hampshire from Ulster, and they accounted for a tenth of the colony's population.

A New Hampshire family's small settlement in the Ipswich woods beside Millstream is captured in this painting by New Hampshire artist William J. Kaula.

With the towns growing crowded and the surrounding woods all but emptied of native inhabitants, settlement began to expand. Samuel Lane wrote in 1748,

NEW HAMPSHIRE
circa 1765

- New Hampshire colony
- Disputed by New Hampshire & New York colony
- Massachusetts Bay colony
- ········ Proclamation line of 1763
- —— Colony boundary
- ⊡ Fort
- • Town
- ▲ Mountain
- (Derryville) Historic name

miles
0   20   40

QUEBEC (CANADA)

ISLAND OF NEWFOUNDLAND (CAN.)

NEW BRUNSWICK (CAN.)

MAINE

NOVA SCOTIA (CAN.)

Area of main map
NEW HAMPSHIRE

NEW YORK

VT.

N.H.

CONN.

R.I.

MASS.

PENN.

MD.

N.J.

VA.

DEL.

N.C.

ATLANTIC OCEAN

Present-day boundaries shown

QUEBEC

PROVINCE OF MAINE
(Part of Massachusetts 1677 to 1820)

Androscoggin River

Reserved for Indians

• Colebrook

• Lancaster

Connecticut River

• Lisbon
• Franconia

Mount Washington
1,917m (6,288ft)

WHITE MTS.

• Woodsville

• Lincoln

Pemigewasset R.

• Conway

Saco River

• Haverhill

• Warren

• Orford

• Sandwich

Lake Winnipesaukee

• Hanover
• Enfield • Canaan
• Lebanon

• Meredith

• Wolfeboro (Wolfsboro)

Lake Wentworth

New Salisbury (Bakers Town)

NEW HAMPSHIRE COLONY

Salmon Falls River

• New London

• Newport

Merrimack River

• Canterbury

Cocheco River

• Charlestown

• Concord

• Somersworth

• Dover

• Durham

Piscataqua R.

Portsmouth (Strawbery Banke)

• Hillsboro (Hillsborough)

(Oyster River Plantation)

• Walpole

• Suncook

• Newmarket

• Raymond

⊡ Castle William and Mary

Rye (Odiorne's Point)

• Keene

• Manchester (Derryville)

Squamscott R.

• Exeter

Great Bay

• North Hampton

• Peterborough

• Merrimack

• Kingston

• Hampton

• Wilton

• Londonderry

• Newton

• Hinsdale

• Winchester (Arlington)

• Jaffrey

• Milford (Monson)

• Salem

• Plaistow

ATLANTIC OCEAN

• Dunstable

MASSACHUSETTS COLONY

NEW YORK COLONY

Hudson River

Present-day shorelines shown

The end of the Indian wars encouraged settlement and the growth of towns in New Hampshire. The greatest growth came under the governorships of Benning Wentworth and his nephew John. By 1765, there were more than 200 towns, mostly along the major river valleys and within 40 miles of the Atlantic Ocean. The Proclamation boundary (dotted line on the map) reserved land to the west for Native Americans. Much of what is now Vermont was claimed by New Hampshire and New York.

"*There is an uncommon stir among people this fall after lands in the woods.*" Lane, who had training as a surveyor, was involved in laying out several new towns in New Hampshire. An entry in his journal for November that same year says, "*I set out with the Exeter people to lay out a town on ye west side of Pemigawassut River above Bakers Town. This is the first time I camp'd in ye woods.*" By the 1760s, the number of towns in New Hampshire had grown from four to 150.

As trade expanded, New Hampshire began printing its own money. In 1756, a Boston printer named Daniel Fowle moved to Portsmouth and founded the *New Hampshire Gazette*. As ads for goods and services began appearing in newspapers, demand for services increased and so did the colony's

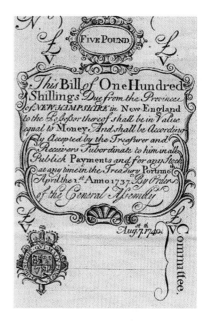

An example of a 100 shilling New Hampshire note, dated August 7, 1740.

prosperity. By the 1760s, visitors to New Hampshire remarked upon its many fine mansions and well-built churches and public buildings. The towns were filled with sturdy frame houses, taverns, breweries, marketplaces, and shops and surrounded by well-tended, fenced-in fields. Some families, such as the Wentworths, Vaughns, and Waldrons, accumulated enormous fortunes. They built huge homes in Portsmouth, sponsored concerts and plays,

Benning Wentworth

Benning Wentworth was born in 1696. He was the eldest son of Lieutenant Governor John Wentworth of New Hampshire and his wife, Sarah. He graduated from Harvard in 1715 and married Abigail Ruck in Boston in 1719. They had several children together, but all of them died before their father did.

Wentworth became governor of New Hampshire in 1741 and served until 1767, longer than any other colonial royal governor. To raise money for community projects, he pioneered the use of lotteries. To keep the residents of New Hampshire happy, he was very lax about enforcing unpopular royal decrees, such as the Navigation Acts, and rules about cutting trees for the masts for ships.

Wentworth used his office to accumulate a vast fortune. He put friends in powerful positions and often took cash payments in exchange. Whenever he made grants of land for new townships, he always awarded himself 500 acres (200 ha). As the townships grew, so did the value of his land. Eventually, he owned more than 100 square miles (260 sq km) of very valuable land.

had their portraits painted, and hosted lavish dances. They also dominated New Hampshire politics.

In 1717, John Wentworth was appointed lieutenant governor. He ran New Hampshire with very little resistance from inside or outside the colony until he died in 1730. A decade later, perhaps because issues with Massachusetts had faded into memory, the Crown no longer saw the need for Massachusetts and New Hampshire to share the same governor. In 1741, John's son Benning Wentworth was appointed the royal governor of New Hampshire In 1767, Benning's nephew John became the third generation of Wentworths to govern New Hampshire. ✾

CHAPTER EIGHT

Revolutionary New Hampshire

NEW HAMPSHIRE RESIDENTS SUPPORT *independence,*
but little military action takes place in their colony.
Royal authority falls apart in 1775.

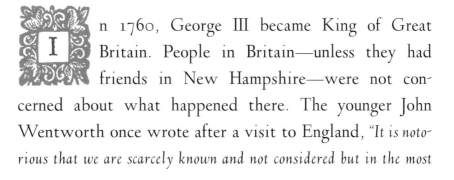 n 1760, George III became King of Great Britain. People in Britain—unless they had friends in New Hampshire—were not concerned about what happened there. The younger John Wentworth once wrote after a visit to England, *"It is notorious that we are scarcely known and not considered but in the most*

OPPOSITE: British Captain John Cochran surrenders to Major John Sullivan after the Americans take control of the fort at Castle William and Mary in Portsmouth in December 1774.

diminutive way, and as a province . . . [we] have no rights or interests."
Despite this apparent neglect, the New Hampshire colony
prospered. By 1775, more than 75,000 people lived there.
The Wentworth governors were at least partly responsible
for that success. Even so, their political influence would
not last. The American Revolution would play a part in
their downfall. Politics back in Britain were also influ-
encing New Hampshire.

BRITISH TAXES

The new king ordered his officials in Britain to make sure
that the royal governors in America began following the
orders of Parliament much more carefully. British laws,
however, including taxes levied from Britain, were often
made by people who knew very little about the situation in
New Hampshire. John Wentworth's uncle and grandfather
had usually ignored instructions from the Crown that they
thought were harmful to the colony. People expected John
to do the same, but the king was making that impossible.
When Wentworth tried to enforce George III's unpopular
regulations, people became so angry that they threw rocks
at the windows of his house.

In 1765, the British Parliament passed the Stamp Act.
The Stamp Act required that paper items such as legal doc-
uments, newspapers, and even playing cards had to have a
special stamp. A person had to pay a tax to the government

to get the stamp. This law was extremely unpopular. On April 11, 1766, Samuel Lane wrote, *"I was sworn a Justice of the Peace. A great uproar in the country about the Stamp Act."* Protesters in towns throughout the American colonies, including Portsmouth, organized themselves into groups called the Sons of Liberty to fight the Stamp Act. When it became clear in Britain that the Stamp Act was not being

enforced, the Townshend Acts were passed to replace it. Taxes on everyday products such as lead, paper, paint, glass, and tea were ordered. Samuel Lane, often sympathetic to royal causes, did not view the new laws as an improvement: *"Duties laid on glass, tea, paper, etc. at home; makes uneasiness here. Money scarce is the general complaint."*

A picture of a stamp colonists were forced to purchase and affix to all printed materials as ordered by the Stamp Act, passed by Parliament in 1765.

Great change was afoot throughout the British colonies of North America. While Boston, Massachusetts, was at the center of unrest, it was by no means unique. Everywhere, colonists were beginning to perceive themselves as American instead of British. New Hampshire and other Colonies had been left alone to rule themselves for a long time, and they had prospered and grown strong. From the colonists' point of view, it seemed that the British government now wanted to control the Colonies and take their profits without having earned them.

A straw dummy of a Stamp Act official is hanged in effigy
by colonists protesting the tax.

COMMITTEES OF CORRESPONDENCE

In May 1772, the New Hampshire assembly received letters from Virginia and Rhode Island asking it to create a Committee of Correspondence, to be responsible for keeping in touch with the other Colonies about the worsening situation with Britain. Wentworth's attempts to argue against the committee angered residents. The assembly sent word back that a Committee of Correspondence had been created.

By 1772, Parliament had repealed the Townshend Acts, bowing to pressure from a boycott against British goods that began in Boston. Parliament then passed the Tea Act, putting a tax on tea, which nearly everyone in the Colonies drank. The tax caused a tremendous outcry in America. In Boston, Patriots disguised as Indians threw a shipment of tea into the harbor rather than pay the tax. Many in New Hampshire recorded the event:

Patriot—a colonist who favored independence from Britain

1773—*What is most remarkable . . . is the great tumults about the duty on tea, sent here by the East India Company; 342 chests of it being thrown into the sea at Boston.*

May, 1774— *. . . great commotion in the whole nation and this land about the tea that was destroyed in Boston. . . . by an act of Parliament, the Port of Boston is shut up.*

New Hampshire residents looked on what came to be called the Boston Tea Party with admiration, and Portsmouth and other towns passed resolutions that the Tea Act should not be obeyed. When a large shipment of tea arrived in Portsmouth in 1774, Wentworth warned that he could not guarantee the ship captain's safety. Only the fact that the tea was sent back immediately prevented violence. The governor's control was all but gone.

NEW HAMPSHIRE SUPPORTS INDEPENDENCE

After the Boston Tea Party, Britain punished the rebellious city by closing its port and quartering large numbers of British troops in the city under the command of General Thomas Gage. In response, New Hampshire residents sent goods and supplies overland to their blockaded neighbors.

In 1773, General Gage tried to have barracks built to house his troops in Boston, but local carpenters refused to do the work. Gage asked Wentworth to send New Hampshire carpenters to do the job. Wentworth agreed to the request, but tried to keep the affair secret. He quietly hired men who lived near his country estate without telling them what they were being hired to do. His attempt at secrecy didn't work. Soon, everyone knew what he had done, and at least one group in Portsmouth called him *"an enemy . . . to the community."* People throughout New Hampshire were so furious that they attacked several royal officials in 1774. Wentworth began to fear for his personal safety.

Two months later, Paul Revere, a Boston silversmith who would later become famous for carrying word of the British advance toward Lexington and Concord, rode into Portsmouth carrying a message from Boston. British troops were on their way. They intended to take control of a fort called Castle William and Mary that protected Portsmouth Harbor, seizing any weapons and ammunition that the colonists had stored there and might use against the troops. New Hampshire's reaction would remove any doubt about the colonists' willingness to resist the king's government.

ROYAL AUTHORITY FALLS APART

On December 14 , 400 New Hampshire residents with the help of Provincial Militia Major John Sullivan, stormed the fort and secured the weapons and ammunition stored there. They loaded the material into small boats and moved it all to hiding places in the surrounding towns. The governor was powerless to stop them. When he ordered the militia into action, the militia refused to obey. When he appealed to local officials to back him up, they refused. Even the crew of his own boat refused to take him out to the fort. By the time two British warships arrived at the fort, all the munitions had been removed and hidden.

The British flag flies at the entrance of Portsmouth Harbor,
site of the fort at Castle William and Mary.

After the raid on Castle William and Mary, royal
authority in New Hampshire began to fall apart. Royal
officials were harassed until they either resigned their posts
or fled the colony. The militia refused to obey officers who
seemed to be on the royal side and in several cases simply
chose new officers who embraced the Patriots' cause.
Governor Wentworth became frightened enough to ask
General Gage for British troops to protect him.

On April 19, 1775, British troops encountered armed
resistance in the Massachusetts towns of Lexington and
Concord, taking heavier losses than the commanders had

thought possible. The fighting at Lexington and Concord was the beginning of the American Revolution. Both Samuel Lane and Abner Sanger record the battle, showing that it had impressed all levels of New Hampshire society. Lane wrote,

> A number of regular troops began hostilities at Lexington & Concord; kill'd 8 or 10, of the people in those towns in the battle & wounded many more . . . also kill'd & wounded many of other towns in their retreat: this alaram'd the whole continent; and a large army was soon rais'd & sent to Cambridge for the defense of these colonies, under General Washington.

The day after the fighting, Sanger apparently took time off from working to talk to his fellow townsmen:

> Now is news of the fight with regulars in Concord, Lexington . . . and also of people being killed. Keane town is in an uproar. They want a muster. I go to Baker's, Dorman's, William's office, Wadsworth's, and to his shop, old Gideon Ellis', then to Israel Houghton', then set out home . . . I meet El above the Bellows's house going to hear the news. The night is fair and clear.

The next day, Abner Sanger borrowed a gun and joined the muster of New Hampshire residents who marched to Boston to defend the city against the British. A week later, on April 28, after a rainy march, he recorded his impressions of Boston:

*This morning I got up from my lodging on the hay scaffold.
Fair, clear, and pleasant. Afternoon . . . I go off to a hill in
Charleston called Winter Hill where [I] took a fair view of
Boston and etc., of the Regular's tents, and of the man-of-
war. . . . Also hear the bells ring in Boston, either for joy or
sorrow. Very clear, cold winds from the sea. We see several
vessels off at sea.*

Two months later, units from the New Hampshire
militia fought in what would be called the Battle of Bunker
Hill, even though it was fought on Breed's Hill.

Governor Wentworth stayed in New Hampshire until
one night in June 1775, shortly after the militia had
marched to Massachusetts. He was having dinner in his
mansion with his friend John Fenton, a known Loyalist
who often spoke out against independence. A mob of local
Patriots showed up to arrest Fenton. At first, Wentworth
refused to give Fenton up, but the mob set up cannon and
prepared to fire at the house. Fenton surrendered, and
Wentworth was ordered to leave Portsmouth with his
family immediately or face arrest. In a letter later written
by Mrs. Wentworth to a friend, she describes *"we did with
great haste."* That very evening, Wentworth took his wife
and five-month-old son to Castle William and Mary,
where they were protected by British warships. When
the ships departed, Wentworth and his family were
aboard. He never returned to New Hampshire. Neither did
royal authority.

New Hampshire was very fortunate in the Revolutionary War. While many New Hampshire men marched off to fight in the war, the raid on Castle William and Mary was the only battle fought on New Hampshire soil. That's not to say the war did not affect New Hampshire. In October 1775, Lane recorded that the residents of Portsmouth were evacuating the city in fear of a British attack: *"The Regulars burnt the town of Falmouth [in Maine] . . . upon which the people of Portsmouth remov'd into the country at a vast expense, expecting to share the same fate very soon, & the province immediately in great numbers went to building fortifications in the Harbor of Portsmouth."* Not until March 1776, when the British left Boston, did the residents of Portsmouth return. And while the war never did reach them, there was always the sense that it wasn't far away: *"August 16, 1777—Fair and warm. . . . I reap wheat on Colonel Hunt's hill. Afternoon we turn and take up and stack. Cannon are heard all afternoon toward the westward."*

SELF-RULE

New Hampshire was well prepared to govern itself. The province had been without executive authority on several occasions in the past and had always managed well. Local authority continued to function, and by January 1776, the House of Representatives had written a constitution for itself. It thus became the very first colony to form its own

John Stark

John Stark served as a general in the Continental Army during the American Revolution. His success leading the First Militia of New Hampshire at the Battle of Bennington in Vermont (below) helped lead to the surrender of the British at Saratoga, New York.

Born in Londonderry, New Hampshire, in 1728, Stark gained the respect of the local Native Americans when he spent time as their prisoner in 1752. Later released, Stark gained military experience fighting in the French and Indian War. In 1775, he led New Hampshire men at the Battle of Bunker (Breed's) Hill, where his Minutemen provided reinforcement for the Continental Army troops there. Impressed with his performance, General George Washington offered Stark a command in the Continental Army.

His words "Live free or die," written in 1809 to a group of men who had fought bravely at Bennington, became the motto for the state of New Hampshire in 1945.

government, completely independent of Britain. Well before the Continental Congress in Philadelphia declared American independence from Britain, New Hampshire already had a stable, functioning government that most of its people approved of.

When the Continental Congress in Philadelphia did convene in the hot summer of 1776, New Hampshire sent Josiah Bartlett and Matthew Thornton, both doctors, and William Whipple, who would become a general in the Continental Army, as delegates. All three cast votes in favor of independence.

Although there were some Loyalists, most in New Hampshire supported the break with royal authority. That independence and pride are present today in the state of New Hampshire, whose motto is John Stark's words: "Live Free or Die." ❈

TIME LINE

1603 Martin Pring goes ashore in New Hampshire and later builds a fort in Massachusetts. John Smith maps the New England coastline. The Council for New England is created.

1622 Captain John Mason and Sir Ferdinando Gorges receive grants to New Hampshire and Maine.

1623 David Thompson arrives in Piscataqua and builds Pannaway House.

1629 New Hampshire is named by Captain John Mason, who sends an expedition to the new territory led by Walter Neale.

1630 Great House is built at Strawbery Banke.

1633 Dover is founded.

1637 Exeter is founded.

1638 Hampton is founded.

1641 The Massachusetts General Court extends its authority over Dover.

1643 The Massachusetts General Court extends its authority over Exeter.

1650 Joseph Mason brings a lawsuit over his land claims in the Massachusetts General Court.

1651 Strawbery Banke petitions the Massachusetts General Court to become part of Massachusetts.

1652 New Hampshire is now under Massachusetts's control.

1674 The Committee on Trade and Plantations (the Lords of Trade) is established.

1679 Massachusetts is ordered to withdraw from New Hampshire.

1680 New Hampshire is made a royal colony.

1685 The Massachusetts charter is revoked. New Hampshire is placed within the Dominion of New England.

1690 New Hampshire is again placed under Massachusetts's control.

1692 New Hampshire is again made a royal colony under Governor Samuel Allen.

1713 The Treaty of Utrecht is signed in Europe.

1741 Benning Wentworth becomes governor of New Hampshire.

1765 Parliament passes the Stamp Act.

1767 John Wentworth becomes governor of New Hampshire. Parliament repeals the Stamp Act and passes the Townshend Acts.

1772 Parliament passes the Tea Act. Committees of Correspondence are established throughout the Colonies.

1774 New Hampshire colonists take control of Castle William and Mary and hide munitions stored there from the British.

1775 British troops and colonial militia fight at Lexington and Concord. Governor Wentworth leaves New Hampshire, ending royal authority there. New Hampshire militia, commanded by John Stark, fight the British on Breed's Hill.

1776 The newly formed New Hampshire House of Representatives ratifies the New Hampshire constitution. The Colonies form the United States and declare themselves independent of Great Britain.

RESOURCES

BOOKS

Brown, Jerald E. and Donna-Belle Garvin. *The Years of the Life of Samuel Lane, 1718-1806: A New Hampshire Man and His World.* Hanover, New Hampshire: University Press of New England, 2000.

Fradin, Dennis Brindell. *The Signers.* New York: Walker, 2002.

Simmons, R.C. *The American Colonies: From Settlement to Independence.* New York: W.W. Norton, 1976.

Taylor, Alan. *American Colonies: The Settling of North America.* New York: Penguin Books, 2002.

Thompson, John M. *The Revolutionary War.* Washington, D.C.: National Geographic, 2004.

WEB SITES

American Journeys
http://www.americanjourneys.org/
Digital archive of eyewitness accounts of early exploration.

Explorers and Settlers of North America
http://oz.plymouth.edu/~lts/wilderness/explorers.html
Summaries of the lives of various early explorers.

Geocities
http://www.geocities.com/bigorrin/abenaki kids.htm
Kids' web site about the Abenaki.

Living History Museum
http://www.fortat4.com/index.php
Web site of the Living History Museum in Charlestown, New Hampshire.

The New Hampshire Historical Society
http://www.nhhistory.org/index.html
Web site of the New Hampshire Historical Society in Concord, New Hampshire.

Strawbery Banke Museum
http://www.strawberyBanke.org/
Web site of the Strawbery Banke Museum in Portsmouth.

QUOTE SOURCES

CHAPTER ONE
p. 19 "pierce...the land," Burrage, Henry S. (editor). *The Voyage of Martin Pring, 1603.* New York: Charles Scribner's Sons, 1906, p. 346; p. 20 "great and...[Mastiffs]." Burrage, p. 348; " be rid of...flee away." Burrage, p. 348; "we beheld...sharpe noses." Burrage, p. 346; "signes of...had beene" Burrage, p. 346; "certaine...together" Burrage, p. 346; "abandoned...Savages." Burrage, p. 346; p. 21 Their Boats...very swiftly." Burrage, p. 348; p. 22 "We beheld...wild fruits." Burrage, p. 349.

CHAPTER TWO
p. 26 "Could I...than anywhere." Winslow, Ola Elizabeth. *Portsmouth: The Life of A Town.* New York: Macmillan, 1966, p. 21; p. 29 "I will not...through them." Daniell, Jere R. *Colonial New Hampshire.* Millwood, New York: KTO Press, 1981, p. 21; "But certainly,...be diligent." Daniell, p. 21; p. 34 "If there were...reimbursed again." Daniell, pp. 24–25.

CHAPTER THREE
p. 39 "usual manner...us to them." Daniell, Jere R. *Colonial New Hampshire.* Millwood, New York: KTO Press, 1981, p. 31; p. 44 "of the want...and commonwealth." Daniell, p. 41; p. 46 "nothing left...of ruin." Daniell, p. 43.

CHAPTER FOUR
p. 51 "Haste! Post Haste!" Daniell, Jere R. *Colonial New Hampshire.* Millwood, New York: KTO Press, 1981, p.69.

CHAPTER FIVE
p. 58 "Small is...principal delight." Daniell, Jere R. *Colonial New Hampshire.* Millwood, New York: KTO Press, 1981, p. 166; "Young people...their

parents." Daniell, p. 167; p. 59 "Every man must...did enter." Hawke, David Freeman. *Everyday Life in Early America.* New York: Harper & Row, 1988, p. 34; p. 63 "You know our...shall be starved." Taylor, Alan. *American Colonies: The Settling of North America.* New York: Penguin Books, 2002, p. 193; "The times are...is entirely gone." Taylor, p. 203; p. 64 "1748—We had...in the woods." Lane, Samuel. *A Journal for the Years 1739–1803.* Concord, New Hampshire: New Hampshire Historical Society, 1937, p. 68; "1749—Most disturbing drought...to live on." Lane, pp. 68–69; p. 66 1743–Indians...by the Indians." Lane, p. 30; p. 67 "John Church, sen....carried away." Daniell, p. 110; "such a scarcity...handful of corn." Lane, p. 70; "There are no...we know of." Daniell, p. 138.

CHAPTER SIX
p. 71 "My name is Walter." Daniell, Jere R. *Colonial New Hampshire.* Millwood, New York: KTO Press, 1981, p.84; p. 73 "I esteem it...in execution." Daniell, p. 95; p. 74 "ruled, swayed...at their pleasure." Daniell, p. 70; "ancient and infirm." Daniell, p. 79.

CHAPTER SEVEN
p. 83 "Town Meeting Day...Tything man." Brown, Jerald E. *The Years of the Life of Samuel Lane, 1718–1806.* Hanover, New Hampshire: University Press of New England, 2000, p. 66; "El to town...Stormy night," Stabler, Lois K., editor. *Very Poor and of a Lo Make: The Journal of Abner Sanger.* Portsmouth, New Hampshire: Peter E. Randall, 1986, p. 28; "This is Town Meeting Day." Stabler, p. 30; pp. 83–84 "Fair north-west winds...Grows cold." Stabler,

p. 75; p. 84 "I go up to...see the mob." Stabler, pp. 19–20; "I go up to Captain...until midnight." pp. 41–42; "The course of...this continent." Lane, Samuel. *A Journal for the Years 1739–1803.* Concord, New Hampshire: New Hampshire Historical Society, 1937, p. 45; p. 87 "There is an...in the woods." Brown, p. 81; "I set out...in ye woods." Lane, p. 33.

CHAPTER EIGHT
pp. 91–92 "It is notorious...rights or interests." Daniell, Jere R. *Colonial New Hampshire.* Millwood, New York: KTO Press, 1981, pp. 218–219; p. 93 "I was sworn...Stamp Act." Lane, Samuel. *A Journal for the Years 1739–1803.* Concord, New Hampshire: New Hampshire Historical Society, 1937, p.40; "Duties laid on...general complaint." Lane, p. 78; p. 95 "1773–What is most...is shut up." Lane, p. 80; p. 96 "an enemy...to the community." Daniell, p. 233; p. 99 "A number...General Washington." Lane, p. 45; "Now is news...fair and clear." Stabler, Lois K., editor. *Very Poor and of a Lo Make: The Journal of Abner Sanger.* Portsmouth, New Hampshire: Peter E. Randall, 1986, pp. 35–36; p. 100 "This morning I...off at sea." Stabler, pp. 38–39; p. "we did with great haste." http://www.nhssar. org/essays/FortConstitution.htm, Section VII; p. 101 "The Regulars burnt...Harbor of Portsmouth." Lane, p. 46; "August 16, 1777...toward the westward." Stabler, p. 152.

INDEX

Boldface indicates
illustrations.

Abenaki Indians 19
  assisting settlers 29
  conflict with colonists 63,
    64–67
  farming 42
  trade with settlers 33
Algonquian Indians
  14–15, 19, 20, 21, 55
Allen, Samuel 78–79,
  81–82
American Revolution **9**,
  72, 98–101, 102
Anthropologist
  definition 15
Assembly (governmental
  body) 54, 71, 82, 95
Asset
  definition 34

Barefoote, Walter 71
Bartlett, Josiah 103
Batchellor, Stephen 41–42
Bellingham, Richard 51
Bellomont, Lord 82
Bennington, Battle of 102,
  102
Birch-bark canoes **12**, 21
Boston, Mass.
  conflicts with Great
    Britain 93, 95–96,
    99–100
Boston Tea Party 95–96
Brereton, John 18
Bunker Hill, Battle of
  (1775) 91, 100, 102

Cabot, John 16
Canoes
  birch-bark **12**, 21
Castle William and Mary,
  Portsmouth, N.H. **90**,
  97, **98**, 100
Charles, Prince (England)
  26
Charles II, King (England)
  48, 49–50, 52–53, 75
Children 58
Church, John 67
Church of England
  Common Prayer book **48**
Cochran, John **90**
Colman, Samuel
  artwork by **56**
Colonists
  challenges 10
  conflicts with Great
    Britain 93–97

conflicts with Indians
  10–11, 63, 64–67, **65**
early settlements 17,
  26–27
Committee of
  Correspondence 95
Committee on Trade and
  Plantations 53
Continental Army 91, 102,
  103
Continental Congress 103
Continental Navy 9, **9**
Council for New England
  27, 31
Court system 43–44, 73
Cranfield, Edward 71, 73
Cutt, John 46, 54, 69, 71,
  74
Cutt, Richard 46, 74
Cutt, Robert 74

Dartmouth College
  founding 80
Discoverer (ship) 18, 19
Dogs 20, **20**
Dominion of New England
  76, 78
Dover, N.H.
  conflicts with Abenaki
    Indians 65, 66–67
  government 40, 44, 45,
    51, 54
  home building **36**
  sawmills 61
  settlement 40, 43
  see also Hilton's Point,
    N.H.

Elizabeth I, Queen
  (England) 17
England
  exploration and dis-
    covery 16, 17–18,
    22–23, 24
  government **48**
  map of land claims 2–3
  opinions about colonies
    91–92
Exeter, N.H.
  founder **45**
  government 44, 45, 51, 54
  settlement 41, 43
Exports 61, 62

Family life 57–58
Farming 10, **56**, **57**, 58–60,
  64
Fenton, John 100
Fishing 11, **16**, 16–17, 25
Fishmonger
  definition 29

Foole (dog) 20
Forests 60–61, **61**
Fowle, Daniel 87
France
  alliance with Native
    Americans 11, 64–65
  exploration and
    discovery 17
  map of land claims 2–3
Fur trade 31

Gage, Thomas 96, 98
Gallant (dog) 20
Garrison houses 66
George III, King (Great
  Britain) 91, 92
Gibbins, Ambrose 33, 34
Glorious Revolution 77–78
  playing cards **77**
Gorges, Sir Ferdinando 27,
  30, 30–31, 34
Gosnold, Bartholomew
  17–18
Great House, Strawbery
  Banke, N.H. 33
  map 35
Great Island, N.H. 19, 29,
  43, 47
Gristmills 60

Halifax, H.M.S. (ship) **9**
Hampton, N.H. 42, 43, 45,
  51, 54
Heresy
  definition 41
Hilton, Edward 29–30
Hilton brothers 40
Hilton's Point, N.H. 30, 35,
  40, 43
  see also Dover, N.H.
House of Representatives
  82, 101
Houses
  building **36**
  wigwams 15, 20
Hutchinson, Anne 41

Investor
  definition 34
Ipswich woods, N.H.
  family settlement **85**
Iroquois, Lake of the 31,
  32, 34

James II, King (England)
  75, 75–76, **77**, 77–78
Jamestown, Va. 26

Kaula, William J.
  painting by **85**
Keene, N.H. 83, 84, 99
King's Privy Council 53

Laconia Company 31, 34
Lake of the Iroquois 31, 32,
  34
Lane, Samuel
  report of American
    Revolution 99, 101
  report of conflicts with
    Indians 66
  report of government 83,
    84
  report of hardships
    63–64, 67
  report of taxes 93
  report of town growth 85,
    87
Leader, Richard 46–47
Leveredge, William 40
Levett, Christopher 28–29
Lexington and Concord,
  Battle of (1775) 98–99
Logging **61**, 62, 88
Londonderry, N.H. 85
Lords of Trade
  Massachusetts govern-
    ment 53–54, 75–76,
    82
  New Hampshire govern-
    ment 53–54, 69, 71,
    73, 79, 82
Lotteries 88
Lumber industry 60–61

Maine
  government 11
  patent 34, 52
Maps
  Great House, Strawbery
    Banke, N.H. 35
  New England 24
  New Hampshire bound-
    aries 8
  New Hampshire towns
    86
  North America 2–3
  Royal Colony of New
    Hampshire 55
Mary II, Queen (England)
  77–78
Mason, Anne 46
Mason, John **30**, 30–31,
  33, 34, 35, 46
Mason, Joseph 46
Mason, Robert Tufton 50,
  52, 53, 54
Mason family 46–47, 51,
  78

Massachusetts
  border 50—51
  control of Maine 11
  control of New
      Hampshire 39—45,
      47, 50—54, 78, 81
  government 53—54,
      81—82
  laws 39, 43—44
  relationship with New
      Hampshire 10, 11,
      37—39
  religion 39
  settlers 37—38
Massachusetts Bay Colony
    charter 76
Massachusetts General
    Court 43—45, 46—47
Masts 62, 88
Meeting houses **51**
Mills 60—61
Millstream, N.H. **85**
Mitchell, John
  maps by 8
Mohegan Indians 63
Money 87, **87**

Narragansett Indians 63
Native Americans
  birch-bark canoes **12**, 21
  conflicts with colonists
      10—11, **65**, 66—67
  farming 22
  fear of dogs 20
  French allies 11, 64—65
  trade 26, 33
Natural resources **11**,
      28—29, 60—61, **61**
Naval stores 62
  definition 62
Navigation Acts **68**,
      69—73, 88
Neale, Walter 31, 34
New England
  definition 14
  government 27, 76, 78
  map 24
New Hampshire
  control by Massachusetts
      39—45, 47, 50—54, 78,
      81
  governors 71, 79, 88, 89
  growth 84—85, 87, 92
  local rule 82—84
  maps 8, 35, 55, 86
  motto 102, 103
  naming 31
  patent 52, 53
  relationship with
      Massachusetts 10, 11,
      37—39

royal authority 54,
    75—76, 97—98, 100
self-rule 101, 103
settlers 37—38
state seal 11
Newfoundland, Canada
  fishing **16**, 16—17, 25
Newichawannock Falls,
    N.H. 33, 34, 35, 43,
    46—47
Newmarket, N.H. 66
Nichols, Richard 50—52
Nichols Commission
    50—52, 53
North America
  map 2—3

Palisade
  definition 14
Pannaway House, N.H.
    28—29, 31, 34, 35, 43
Parliament, British 50
  definition 50
Patents 27, 30—31, 52, 53,
    54
  definition 17
Patriots 100
  definition 95
Petition
  definition 47
Pike, John 66—67
Piscataqua, N.H. 27, 29,
    38, 39
  see also Portsmouth,
      N.H.; Strawbery
      Banke, N.H.
Piscataqua River, N.H.-
    Me.
  discovery 19
  maps 35, 55, 86
Pittman, Joseph 67
Plantation
  definition 28
Playing cards **77**
Plymouth Colony, Mass.
    26, 27, 37, 43
Portsmouth, N.H. **38**
  American Revolution 97,
      101
  attacks by Indians 65
  government 47, 51, 52,
      54, 74
  harbor **70**, **98**
  newspaper 87
  shipbuilding 9, 62—63
  smuggling 70, 71, 72
  tax protests 96
  see also Piscataqua, N.H.;
      Strawbery Banke,
      N.H.
Pring, Martin 18—20, 21,
    22—23, 55
Provincial Council 54, 74

Puritans
  beliefs 42
  definition 26
  Dominion of New
      England 76, 78
  influence in New
      Hampshire 39—42,
      43, 52, 73, 82
  influence in North
      America 49—50
  meeting house **51**
  Plymouth colony 26, 37
  punishment **40**
  religious freedom 37, 39,
      42

Randolph, Edward 53,
    70—71
Ranger (ship) **9**
Religious freedom 37, 39,
    42, 52
Revere, Paul 97
Ricker, Maturin 67
Ruck, Abigail 88

Sanger, Abner 83—84,
    99—100
Sanger, El 83—84, 99
Sassafras 18, 19—20, 22
Sawmills 60—61
Scotch-Irish people 84—85
Sherburne, Henry 46
Shipbuilding 9, 62—63, 88
Smith, John **24**, 26
  map by 24
Smuggling 70, 71, 72
Sons of Liberty **90**, 93
Spain
  Empire 13
  map of land claims 2—3
Speedwell (ship) 18, 19, 22,
    23
Stamp Act 92—93
  protests **94**
  stamp **93**
Stark, John 102
Strawbery Banke, N.H.
  government 45—46, 47
  homes 87
  map 35
  settlement 33—34, 35, **38**,
      43, 74
  see also Piscataqua, N.H.;
      Portsmouth, N.H.
Sullivan, John **90**, 97

Taxes
  protests **94**, 95—96
  Stamp Act 92—93
  Tea Act 95—96
  Townshend Acts 93, 95
Tea Act 95—96
Tenant
  definition 46

Thompson, David 27—28
Thornton, Matthew 103
Tidal estuary
  definition 19
Tories
  definition 83
  persecution 83, 84
Town meetings 43, 54, 75,
    83—84
Townshend Acts 93, 95
Trade laws 70, 72, 73
Treaty of Utrecht 67
Tuckerman Ravine, N.H.
    4—5

Vaughn, William 62—63,
    71
Vaughn family 87, 89
Verrazano, Giovanni da 17
Veto
  definition 71
Viceroy
  definition 76
Virginia Company 27

Waldron, Richard 74
Waldron family 87, 89
Warnerton, Thomas 33, 34,
    45—46
Washington, George 102
Washington, Mount, N.H.
    4—5
Wentworth, Benning 88,
    88, 89
Wentworth, John (grand-
    father) 88, 89
Wentworth, John
    (grandson)
  as governor 89, 91, 92, 95,
      96, 98, 100
  and Great Britain 91—92,
      96—97, 98, 100
Wentworth, Sarah 88
Wentworth family 87, 89,
    92, 100
Wheelock, Eleazar **80**
Wheelwright, John 41, 44,
    45
Whigs 83
  definition 83
Whipple, William 103
White Mountains, N.H.
    4—5
Wiggin, Thomas 40
Wigwams 15, 20
William III, King
    (England) 78
Winnacunnet, N.H. 41—42
Winnipesauke, Lake, N.H.
    32
Women's roles 57—58

ABOUT THE AUTHOR AND CONSULTANT

SCOTT AUDEN is a former teacher turned freelance writer. His love of travel has taken him to a variety of countries. This interaction with other cultures coupled with his background in anthropology has stimulated an interest in finding out more about Americans as a people and then sharing his findings through his writings. A graduate of the University of Connecticut, he currently lives in Colchester, Connecticut.

ALAN TAYLOR is a professor of history at the University of California, Davis. He has written several books, including *William Cooper's Town: Power and Persuasion on the Frontier of the Early American Republic*, which won the Pulitzer Prize in American History. His most recent publication is *The Divided Ground: Indians, Settlers, and the Northern Borderland of the American Revolution*. He is also active in the History Project at UC Davis. This project provides curriculum support for K–12 teachers in history and social studies. He lives in Davis, California.

ILLUSTRATION CREDITS